no use

68

NOV 0 8 1984 BRLS   NOV 8 1984

FEB 25 1986 BRLS
              FEB 22 1986 RET

MAR 22 1986 BRLS
                        S/RT APR 17 '86

              APR 24 1986 RET

MAY 15 1995

THE MANAGEMENT OF
DATA PROCESSING

MANAGER'S GUIDE SERIES

The Management of
Data Processing

RICHARD G. CANNING

President, Canning Publications, Inc.,
Vista, California

ROGER L. SISSON

Associate Professor of Operations Research and Industry,
University of Pennsylvania,
Philadelphia, Pennsylvania

John Wiley & Sons, Inc.
New York • London • Sydney

To
WALKER G. STONE
for his friendly encouragement

Series Foreword

In an era in which management science and technology are growing rapidly and at the same time causing great change one thing remains constant—the manager's need to stay informed. To fulfill his need and to master the new techniques, the manager must understand their workings, grasp their potentials and limitations, and know what questions to ask to ensure that a most efficient job will be done.

This is the premise on which the Manager's Guide Series is based and on which each book is written. The subjects are presented in such a manner as to provide ease of understanding, a grasp of terminology, and a comprehension of potential applications. This approach should enable the manager to understand better the techniques of the management sciences and to apply them to his own needs not as a practitioner but as a mature administrator.

Preface

This volume is the second of two books dealing with electronic data processing that we have written for the Manager's Guide Series.

The first volume, *A Manager's Guide to Computer Processing*, describes the relationships between data processing and the other functions of an enterprise—functions such as engineering, marketing, production, and finance. In fact, many of the features of these other functions are found within the data-processing function itself, and a number of the management principles applying to these other functions can be applied to data processing. In addition, the basic principles of data processing, as given in that volume, are of interest at the management level.

The present book complements the first one and deals with the management of data processing *in the years just ahead*. A sudden jump in over-all sophistication in the use of computers has been made with the arrival of the new computers—those being delivered in the last half of the current decade. It is not only the hardware that is causing this increased sophistication—although hardware is an important element—but also the software (the computer programs) and the techniques of use that contribute to this sophistication.

If our assessment of data processing in the not-too-distant future is correct, data processing will have a big impact on the way enterprises are managed. Data processing will be used to aid in managing both the other functions and the enterprise as a whole—by computer-assisted planning, for instance—but, in addition, data processing will take its place alongside the other major functions of the enterprise, that is, alongside engineering, production, finance, and marketing. Top management will become more concerned with the over-all data-processing program, its staffing, and the organization of the data-processing function. This in itself will be a significant change for most managements, because today data processing usually stands well down on the organizational ladder where it receives little attention from executive management. In short, we foresee that data processing will become the "upstart" function within the next few years, as it elbows its way up the ladder, but only by moving up can it carry on the activities that clearly lie ahead for it.

It is not just a case of the other functional segments of the enterprise adjusting to the upstart. The management of data processing itself must change. The management methods that have served data processing in the past will be severely tried by new requirements—and, in our opinion, will be found wanting on all too many occasions. To illustrate this point we have singled out for analysis four basic decision areas within data processing; (a) data-processing project selection and scheduling, (b) organization of the department and its projects, (c) staffing, and (d) selection of equipment, software, and methods. The current methodology, along with its shortcomings, is reviewed for these four decision areas. The major portion of the book then deals with the new requirements for each of these areas and our recommendations on how these requirements can be met.

In this book, then, we have attempted to show the emerging role of data processing in the years just ahead and the adjustments to be made by management to accommodate this new role.

In numerous examples throughout the book we have drawn on material that has appeared in *EDP Analyzer* with the permission of the copyright owner, Canning Publications, Inc.

Richard G. Canning
Roger L. Sisson

Vista, California
Philadelphia, Pennsylvania
April 1967

Contents

I The Past Is Prologue

It appears to us that the transition from the second to the third generation of computers is potentially a greater jump than the transition from tabulating machines to computers or between first- and second-generation computers. Considerable difficulty was experienced in converting to computers in the first place — and we foresee potentially greater difficulties just ahead. Users have gained significant benefits from the computers already installed. But even greater benefits are on the horizon.

This statement about the potential of the new computers may be surprising to some. What it implies is that we really are not "learning to live" with the computers; rather the computer seems to remain tantalizingly just beyond our reach. But is this really so? Are the new computers really that much different from previous ones? And once the conversion to the new computers has been completed, will not the field be able to proceed at a more leisurely pace?

The goal of this book is to assess the impact of the new computers, as we see it, and the challenge that these machines pose for management. In it we hope to show why we think the transition to these new machines will be a larger jump than previous transitions.

DEVELOPMENT OF ELECTRONIC COMPUTERS

Before getting into this subject, though, it would be helpful to look back over the last two decades to see what has transpired in the use of electronic computers. We treat only the highlights of this era, with reflections on experiences and observations. (References to specific supporting literature will be found in the bibliography.)

A major characteristic of the computer field is its rate of growth; it is probably the fastest growing capital goods market in history. The growth rate has averaged close to 25 per cent per year in recent years, and the evidence indicates that this rate will continue. Although the number of computers has increased through what the economists call "extensive cultivation," in which new users install computers, the total *computing power* has increased mainly from "intensive cultivation," in which existing users install more and more powerful computers.

Another major characteristic is the rate of technological change. Three identifiable generations of computers have been observed in a period of time equivalent to less than one human generation. There is no evidence yet that this rate of change will diminish.

The increase in the speed of computation and the decrease in its cost since 1945 provide phenomena almost unparalleled in human history. As Dr. Richard Hamming of Bell Telephone Laboratories pointed out in a recent speech, earliest man probably could walk at the speed of about four miles per hour. Today's commercial jet planes fly at 600 miles per hour, an increase of only 150 times over walking speed. Supersonic jets will fly at about 2000 miles per hour, an increase of 500. Spacecraft are injected into orbit at speeds of 18,000 miles per hour, an increase of 4500. Today's electronic computers, however, will perform computations *several million times* faster than the original Harvard Mark I computer, built in 1944.

A similar phenomenon has occurred in the case of computing costs. The cost of executing a given solution to a problem has decreased several thousand times since 1945. As Dr. Hamming pointed out, if the cost of automobiles had decreased proportionately in this same length of time and we had trouble finding a parking space while going to a baseball game we would not bother — we would just "throw the car away" and buy another after the game.

The trend of increasing speeds and decreasing computation costs is continuing and is expected to continue for at least much of the next decade; no obvious end is in sight for this trend; for example, computation costs have been decreasing to between one third and one fifth of their previous level every three years, as new computers are released. Thus a data processing workload with processing costs of $100 in 1960 could be done for about $25 by 1963. It could be done for about $5 with the arrival of the new third-generation computers in early 1966. Very likely it will be done for about $1 in 1969. As we discuss later, this great decrease in the cost of computation will have a significant effect on the decision areas concerned with data processing.

We should point out here that management does not observe all of these decreases in computation costs in the form of reduced expenses. For one thing, job complexity is increased, as the power to handle increased complexity becomes available. Some operating functions, formerly performed manually — or skipped entirely if a data processing manager wanted to cut corners — have been transferred to the computer, but the fact remains that the costs have been coming down at the rate mentioned.

Another characteristic of the computer field is the often-unrecognized importance of the computer programs and the strides that have been made with programming technology. In the mid-1950's, programming was quite rudimentary. Jobs were programmed in the machine's own language, usually numbers (occasionally binary numbers at that). By the late 1950's the technology had advanced to the point where programmers could write in languages more suitable for humans — such as abbreviated words and mathematical symbols. Translation programs became available for translating the programmer's language to the machine language. Also, generalized programs began to appear, largely eliminating the need for a user to program those particular functions — functions such as sorting and report preparation. During the 1960's much more generalized programs have become available — programs that greatly reduce the effort required for converting new applications to a computer. We have more to say on this point — and its importance to data processing management — later in the book.

Another characteristic of the field is the development of networks of computers — computers that intercommunicate. For much business data it is now not necessary to transmit it between organizations on paper. Instead, data on magnetic tapes may be exchanged or it may be transmitted directly via data communications. Income tax and social security payroll deduction data may be submitted to the government on magnetic tape. Large grocery chains are entering purchase orders with food manufacturers by computer-to-computer communications. A sales agent for one airline can sell seat space on other airlines via his company's computer. The role of paper as a transmission medium for data has decreased — and is expected to decrease even more markedly in the next decade.

Other changes in the computers themselves have affected data processing methodology. The first generation of commercial data processing computers occurred approximately in the time period 1955 to 1960. With our hindsight, we can now classify these machines as slow, with small internal memories, able to work on only one job at a time, and dependent on magnetic tape for the bulk storage of data. These characteristics in turn meant that job programs could not be large, so that management had to look for high-volume jobs that did not require extensive processing logic — payroll, billing, sales analysis, inventory record keeping, etc. The computer was used sequentially — job A was worked to completion, then job B, and so on.

The second generation of computers occurred during the years 1960 to 1965. These machines provided larger internal memories, so that larger, more complex programs could be provided. Magnetic tape was still the primary medium for the storage of data files, but mass storage devices began to see widespread adoption. (Other terms for mass storage devices are random access devices and direct access devices.) Data communications were introduced in which computers could intercommunicate directly. But still the computer was used sequentially, one job at a time.

The third generation of computers began to arrive in 1965, and if the previous pattern holds we should not expect a significantly new generation before 1970. This third generation of computers has much greater internal memory capabilities, and much larger, more complex programs can be written. In addition, these computers exploit a sophisticated *interrupt capability* in new and novel ways — ways that allow the computer to be shared between jobs for short intervals of time. As far as a human observer is concerned, the computer is working on a number of jobs concurrently. Actually, it is working on one job for perhaps a few thousandths of a second and then switches to another job. Another feature of the third-generation computers is the more extensive use of data communications; common data codes are used to facilitate this communication. Mass storage devices are much larger, providing storage of billions of characters of data on-line (automatically available) to the computer, and at costs that are competitive with magnetic tape costs. Cost per character stored on magnetic tape has come down by a factor of 8 since 1955; even so, mass storage costs are catching up. The net result of these changes is that larger jobs can be handled effectively, large files can be stored on mass storage devices, and the computer can easily switch from one job to another as inputs arrive from many sources.

Still other types of changes have occurred that affect management decision areas concerned with data processing. These changes involve the types of job that have been put on the computer. During the first two generations of computers most of the effort has been expended in converting record-keeping operations to the computer. Initial record-keeping operations involved payroll, billing, accounts payable, and such. As more experience was gained, more sophisticated record-keeping operations were implemented — for instance, airline reservation systems where the different airlines' computers could intercommunicate. The Chrysler Corporation has put the records of all automobiles covered by their 50,000-mile warranty program on a computer — and any Chrysler dealer can determine the warranty status of any car in the program in a matter of minutes.

Interest is expanding beyond record keeping operations. The use of management science techniques, coupled with the use of the computer, is finally coming into its own. Although great accomplishments were predicted for these techniques in the early and mid-1950's, they did not receive widespread acceptance. Apparently management was waiting until it had more of the record-keeping operations on the computer before the management sciences were seriously considered. In the 1960's quantitative techniques for inventory control have become widely used — and are given much credit for prolonging the prosperity cycle during the 1960's. Petroleum companies, among others, have obtained substantial benefits from the use of the linear programming technique for scheduling operations. The technique of simulation has proved useful for testing alternative courses of action. The computer is finally beginning to be used to assist in the more complex mental processes.

Research is progressing on using computers for even higher-level mental processes. Examples in this area include medical diagnoses, legal precedent searches, analysis of natural language for meaning, translation between human languages (between Russian and English, say), and monitoring vital patient functions during surgery. Progress in such areas has been sufficient to establish that the computer *does* have a role to play. The computer will surely be applied to higher and higher mental processes in the business world, to aid the decision makers in performing more effectively.

This, then, is a capsule review of what has occurred in the electronic computer field during the last two decades, with most of the progress occurring in the past ten years. The progress is comparable to going from the Model T Ford to supersonic jet transports in ten years' time. The obvious question is asked: how can management effectively direct and control an activity that is as new as mechanized data processing and yet is changing so rapidly? Where can management turn for guidance in so dynamic an area? It is toward the answers to these questions that this book is aimed.

In the remainder of this chapter we review briefly four major decision areas of data processing management:

- Data processing application selection and scheduling, on a project basis.
- Organization of the data processing department and its projects.
- Staffing the data processing function.
- Selection of data processing equipment, software, and methods.

In this review we discuss how these decision areas are currently being handled in many of the organizations that use computers. In addition, we point out some of the shortcomings of today's methods in these four decision areas. This sets the stage for a discussion of what will be required of data processing management during the years ahead.

FOUR MAJOR DECISION AREAS

Project Selection and Scheduling

There are five major levels of data processing projects:

1. Conversion of an established, well-defined application, such as accounts receivable or payroll.
2. Consolidation of several existing applications to form a more inte-

grated system, such as the consolidation of inventory control, material control, order release, and shop control, within a production control system.

3. Development of a common data file to support a number of applications and to provide consistent data for a management information system.

4. Development of a system to provide significantly improved performance in a major on-going segment of the enterprise — for both information processing and the related physical or service operations; an example would be the redesign and standardization of a product line to provide faster customer service, reduced finished goods inventory, simplified data processing, and so on.

5. Development of a new system to achieve a basic mission of the enterprise, such as opening a new production plant or entering a new market.

The first level is concerned with the conversion of established *applications* to the computer — examples of which include payroll, billing, and sales analysis. As we move to the higher levels, the projects get broader and broader, encompassing more than just data-processing activities. At the highest level, the system being designed is concerned with a basic mission of the enterprise and covers far more than data processing. An example of such a project would be the establishment of a new overseas marketing operation, with decisions on markets, products, prices, organization — and information processing.

Based on a thorough review of the literature, in the decade 1955 to 1965, most of the data-processing projects in the United States apparently were of the first level — the conversion of established applications. While the applications were modified, consolidated, and improved the conversion process, still they fitted this definition. Due to the capabilities and the economics of the first two generations of computers, most attention was given to large-volume applications that would consume good quantities of computer time, so as to achieve economic justification. Another requirement during this stage was that the procedural logic involved should not be so great as to tax the internal memory — the program-storing capacity — of the computers. In the typical case, though, this capacity *was* taxed by at least some of the programs, and programmers spent much time redesigning them to make them fit within the machine.

There was some progress made during this decade on the higher level projects, but such cases were the exception. Airlines and savings banks installed fast response systems for providing faster, more accurate customer service. Some manufacturing plants installed integrated production control systems wherein the receipt of a customer order triggered off a series of events culminating in the ordering of materials and purchased goods so as to fulfill customer requirements.

Most companies, however, chose to follow the approach of "let's crawl before we walk." Applications were converted in a sequence dictated largely by immediate potential financial savings. After a series of related applications had been converted, these were redesigned to form a more integrated system — tying islands of mechanization together to form small continents, as it were.

Why did the conversion of applications so heavily dominate the thinking of data processing management during this period? For one thing, applications were concrete and observable; they provided a firm beginning point and a clear goal for the system designers. Their conversion involved less risk for the organization than would one of the higher level projects. With an unknown new tool (the computer) and relatively untested personnel (the EDP system analysts and programmers), management was naturally reluctant to undertake too risky projects.

There was another important reason for this conservatism. The applications proved to be so difficult to convert to a computer — because of the precision of thought needed to program a computer and the flood of changes that became necessary after an application was converted — that management had good reason to be suspicious of the ability of the EDP people to undertake higher level projects. Reports of trials and tribulations of the computer conversions were widespread.

We might concentrate a moment on this subject of system and program changes. In many organizations, when conversion of an application to a computer was first considered, management was of the opinion that once the programs had been written and checked out they would be run for years and that the EDP people would work on something else. In reality, hardly had the new programs started running when changes were needed. To management this seemed to mean that the original study and design had been poorly done. In fact, though, this condition proved to be most difficult to avoid. Some of the changes were requested by line management as they gained experience with the computerized system. Some were normal extensions of the applications: "We have accounts receivable converted for regular accounts, now let's extend it to cover C.O.D. accounts." A point of concern was that many changes proved to be *most* difficult to incorporate, even though they appeared simple to management. The mechanics of changing computer programs, under the conditions imposed by the existing clumsy programming methods, proved to be challenging. Later we discuss developments in programming methods that promise to be powerful for reducing time for both initial programming and revisions.

The net result was that during the period 1955 to 1965 most computer projects for business data processing were of the application (first) level. The projects were selected on an individual basis and largely on the grounds of immediate potential financial savings. The projects were proposed by middle management; top management adopted a judicial role, deciding which projects to approve and counseling the minimization of risk.

As we shall see, this mode of project selection and scheduling has laid a poor foundation on which to build higher level, broader data processing projects.

Organization of the Data Processing Department

Following are some of the ways in which the data processing function has been handled organizationally:

1. The previous tabulating function, often under the controller, absorbs the systems and procedures function to form the data processing function (system analysis, system design, programming, and operations); it usually still reports to the controller and is at the fourth or fifth organizational level.
2. This is similar to the above, except that the systems and procedures function absorbs the tabulating function to form the data processing function.
3. Where neither tabulating nor systems and procedures can absorb the other, two organizational entities develop — data processing operations and data processing systems and programming; they may or may not report upwards to same vice president.
4. In a relatively few cases data processing operations is centralized,

whereas system analysis and programming are decentralized, with each line organization performing its own system work.

5. A new department is created whose manager may be given a title such as Director of Information Services; this director may report to a vice president or, in even uore exceptional cases (to date), to the president.

The most typical situation has been the first, where the tabulating operation (usually located under the controller) absorbs the systems and procedure function and becomes the data processing department still under the controller. In the second alternative, which has not been quite so common, the systems and procedures absorbs the tabulating function. In either case the data processing department has usually remained at the same organization level as the tabulating operation — at either the fourth or fifth level: for example, president–vice president–controller–manager of data processing.

When one function organizationally absorbed another, political in-fighting probably has occurred and one manager has won out over the other. In other cases neither manager might be strong enough to win out over the other — so that two separate organizations exist. Typically, one of these organizational entities is data processing operations (the successor of the old tabulating operation), whereas the other is data processing systems and programming (the old systems and procedures function). In some companies these two groups report to the same executive; in others they report to two different vice presidents.

In any of these situations data processing has remained at a low level. In particular, if the function is divided between two managers, there is no strong impetus to cause the function to be raised organizationally. Regardless of the lip service paid by top executives to "the importance of data processing," the fact remains that it is treated almost routinely by top management when it is at a low organizational level. Its assigned projects tend to be limited to the more routine aspects of the business, furthering the tendency to convert applications rather than to undertake higher level projects.

Whenever a top executive has grasped the concepts of computer-based data processing and has shown imagination in applying these concepts to important company affairs, he has raised the organizational level of data processing. As an indication of this, the manager assumes a new title — Director of Information Services being an example. Under such circumstances, top management begins to see how data processing can be applied to more than routine functions. Data processing management becomes concerned with broader projects and does not limit its work to the conversion of routine applications. This raising of the organizational level has occurred in relatively few cases to date, to our knowledge. It is our contention, as we will discuss more fully in the book, that the organizational level of data processing *must* be raised if it is to deal adequately with the new developments of the field.

Another aspect of organization is the manner in which data processing projects have been organized. The most usual situation has been for the data processing people to conceive a project and then "sell" the project to the affected line management. If the line managers "buy" the idea of the project and top management approves (if indeed they are even consulted), the data processing people assume responsibility for the project. They perform the analysis of the existing system, design of the new system, programming of the computer, development of clerical procedures for the new system — since people are needed to create input documents for the computer and use computer-prepared output documents — and plan the conversion to the new system. The line departments may or may not participate in these activities; the most usual case is that someone from the line department is assigned as liaison to the project.

This approach has worked with some success where data processing management proposes only those projects in which they are highly confident of success (in other words, conservative projects) and in which they have established good relations with the line department. If the line department is not completely sold on the project and the data processing people encounter resistance during system analysis, system design, programming, or conversion, the results can be just short of disastrous.

In other instances the line departments have proposed the projects and have assumed responsibility for design of the new system. The system plans are then turned over to data processing for programming. The result is that the data processing people feel slighted because they are being given only the more routine aspects of the job. Also, there is the good possibility that the line personnel will not be familiar enough with computerized data processing concepts to develop efficient, practical plans from the standpoint of the computer. There is perhaps less likelihood of trouble with this approach, as opposed to the one discussed above (we know of no good statistics to establish this point), for the line personnel are more likely to support the project even if difficulties do develop.

The most successful projects that we have witnessed have been those in which a partnership relationship has been established between the data processing people and line department personnel. Each has contributed its talents to system analysis, system design, perhaps even programming, and conversion. Moreover, line management has assumed over-all responsibility for the success of the project instead of assigning it to the data processing people. We have more to say about this method later.

From an organizational standpoint, then, the data processing function is typically located at a low (fourth or fifth) organization level. At this level it is difficult for the function to undertake the more comprehensive projects; almost by necessity they are limited to the conversion of applications. Also, the way projects have been organized encourages narrowing their scope. If relations are strained between the data processing and line departments (and strains will occur if one or the other is dominating), the environment is not one in which to undertake the broader, riskier projects.

With the types of project that are now on the horizon, top management must pay particular attention to these organizational considerations.

Staffing

An old saw in the data processing field goes like this: "We believe that it is easier to teach our own people, who know our business, how to program a computer than it is to teach our business to computer experts." The end result of this philosophy is that the bulk of the business data processing installations have selected people from within the company, exposed them to a programming training course provided by the computer manufacturer (of one to three weeks duration), and then put them to work on data processing projects. The computer manufacturers have supported this viewpoint because it gives them the chance to provide a well-defined, useful service to the customer. As we shall see, however, this approach causes its share of difficulties.

The recruiting of trained people to meet staff needs has not been so widespread in data processing as it has in engineering and scientific computing. Part of the reason has been that the recruiting of outside people tends to raise salary levels; management has preferred to use people less skilled in data processing but selected from within the company. Also, there has been the feeling that personnel trained in one business environment cannot transfer their training to another business environment — although this belief has been proved erroneous on many occasions.

Another possible means of meeting personnel requirements is to buy personal services from consulting or computer software firms — the latter being firms that specialize in writing computer programs for clients. Although the software firms see a large portion of their future business (*circa* 1970) in business data processing, to date their services have been little used by data processing management.

The upshot is that staff requirements for data processing installations have been met in particular by selecting people from within the company and then training them in computer methods. This process of selection and training is not a one-time affair but periodic or continuous. Some of the personnel prove inadequate for the job and must be replaced; others leave for jobs elsewhere; others are promoted. Also, as more data processing projects are undertaken, more people are needed.

This method of staffing has worked — but it has shortcomings. The selection methods are far from perfect. Usually, programmer aptitude tests are given, and the results are assigned a high weight in the selection process. While such tests are useful, they must be used with caution. Detailed studies have uncovered cases of low correlations (0.1 or 0.2, or even negative correlations) between aptitude test scores and supervisors' ratings of programmer performance; there is a note on this in the bibliography. We have seen instances where personnel from within a company received passing scores on the aptitude tests, were given programming training, and then floundered on important programs. "Floundering" in this case means that they took the better part of a year to write computer programs that should have been done in weeks and their programs performed poorly.

The training that these people receive from the computer manufacturer should be recognized for what it is — training in how to make the computer execute procedures already designed. They simply learn how to speak the language of the computer. They are not taught how to perform the system analysis needed in an EDP study. They are not taught how to structure a solution that makes efficient use of a computer. They are not taught how to design data files for efficient processing as well as for meeting management's needs for special analyses. They are not even taught how to program *well* — how best to structure programs to meet the needs of the particular job. And they are not taught how to analyze manufacturer-supplied computer software so as to remove errors from it or modify it to meet the organization's needs. All they are taught is a new kind of foreign language — the computer's language. This may be a necessary part of their training, but it is far from sufficient. The computer manufacturers actually have been providing far less service in this area than they should.

The shortcomings of this method of staffing do not end there. The programmers who write the company's computer programs may have been selected from within — but they are often younger, junior-level people who really do not know too much about the business. Older, more experienced people, even if capable of doing programming, often consider it beneath them or feel that they have better opportunities where they are. Because of a less than exhaustive system analysis, the programmers usually encounter many unanswered questions when writing a program — along the line of "what should we do if such and such a condition occurs." It is not unusual for the programmers to make rather important operating decisions when they encounter such situations through impatience or lack of appreciation. Perhaps after a few unhappy experiences in trying to get a decision on the handling of a particular situation the programmer will decide that henceforth when such a situation comes up he will just make the decision himself and say nothing about it. Lack of experience in the business penalizes him and the decision he makes may be a poor one — as has happened time after time. Therefore, although selecting people from within theoretically has its advantages, in practice it does not guarantee that they will "know the business."

The results of this method of staffing might have been acceptable during the first and second generation of computers, but with the arrival of the third generation — and the associated developments — a higher level of skills will be needed than this method produces. Later we discuss what these needs are and how they may be met.

Selection of Equipment, Software, and Methods

There are three main systems in use today for selecting equipment, software, and methods — favored manufacturer, bidding, and mechanized evaluation — but even the best of these falls short of what is really desired.

The favored-manufacturer method is, we believe (and somewhat surprisingly), the most widely used. In essence it is as follows. When your favorite computer manufacturer announces a new computer that looks attractive, order it. The computer salesman will then suggest what software to use, such as the programming language. As for the selection of system analysis and design methods, he will point out that this is your decision but he will suggest that your people stick by the old tried-and-true brute-force methods.

The bidding approach is concerned primarily with the selection of equipment, because equipment selection can be reduced to familiar financial terms. Specifications are submitted to the various computer manufacturers who in turn submit bids. The bids may or may not include detailed analyses of times and costs to perform specified workloads. Subtle characteristics of the software are almost always ignored, even though they can have an important bearing on costs. After the computer manufacturer has been selected (perhaps on the basis of the most economical equipment), this method follows the approach of the favored-manufacturer method. The computer salesman recommends the software and methods.

(Do we sound overly critical and perhaps stretching a point? Well, perhaps. Most users would not agree that the above descriptions fit them, but there is more fact than fancy in them, based on our knowledge of scores of installations.)

The mechanized-evaluation approach comes closest to meeting

the needs of the situation. With it, system specifications are set up and then a variety of computer configurations are evaluated against these specifications, *by using a computer.* Here is an obvious application for a computer, but one that has been seldom used. With it, many computer configurations can be evaluated, more than would be feasible when the evaluation is done manually. Moreover, subtle features of the equipment *and the software* can be included in the evaluation. Thus a variety of combinations of hardware and software can be evaluated. There is a much better chance of selecting the combination that fits your requirements by this method than by the two predominant methods described above.

The field is reaching a state in which mechanized evaluations will be a necessity. There are now so many models of computers, so many possible variations in system design, and so many options with software that it is becoming impossible to perform an objective evaluation and selection by manual methods.

To add to the complications, computers are being used for such a variety of tasks that it is becoming difficult to define a "typical workload" to use to evaluate computer systems. Thus the flexibility and growth potential of alternative systems must be examined. This is difficult even with mechanized evaluations.

Growing Complexities of These Decision Areas

So this is where the field stands with the arrival of the third generation of computers. The equipment is much more powerful, it is faster, it can store more data, it can handle multiple jobs at one time. There are many possible combinations of hardware, software, and methods that can be used. The field is achieving the capability of undertaking the higher level, broader projects — and there will be a competitive pressure for organizations to undertake such projects. Simply converting routine applications will not be enough.

The management methods that gave passable performance during the first and second generations of computers will not be adequate for the years immediately ahead. Better decision-making methods are needed — for project selection and scheduling, for organizing, for staffing, and for selecting equipment, software, and methods.

The goal of this book is to explore the subject of the management of data processing in terms of these four decision areas in the environment of the third generation of computers. We discuss what has to be done in each of these areas and include some guidelines that hopefully will assist in the performance of management functions.

2 Choosing the Direction

Data processing management at many installations today is faced with the very difficult task of deciding how to allocate resources to jobs and projects. The backlog of work in a data processing department can be substantial; it is not unusual for a rather small department (say, four to six system analysts and programmers) to have a backlog of two hundred jobs. Some of these jobs are small, of course, such as minor changes to existing programs, but others involve complete new programs.

Not only is data processing management faced with choosing between these jobs already in the backlog, they also have the uncomfortable feeling that there are other more important projects that ought to be considered. They hear about developments in online systems, in data communications, and in new methods for computer input and output. Management recognizes that some attention should be paid to such developments — but with a sizable backlog of projects already confronting them, it is hard to divert resources to investigate these new developments.

So data processing management needs improved methods to help decide where best to allocate their system analyst and programmer resources. In short, they need a better approach to choosing the direction of the company's data processing activities. Their problem is getting more complex by the month as new technological developments occur.

In this chapter we discuss some of these technological developments that are pressing in on data processing management and demanding attention — to show how the "choosing of direction" is becoming more complex. Then we discuss the most effective approach with which we are familiar for guiding a data processing program in the face of so many possible projects.

Pressure from the Technology

In the rapidly moving computer field new technological developments are occurring continually, many of which promise benefits to users of electronic data processing. The problem is, of course, deciding which ones offer the most promise for a particular situation. Here is a brief review of some of the major developments, to illustrate what is occurring in the field.

Fast Response Systems. It was theoretically possible to feed information into a computer as the information was generated — as a sales transaction occurred, for instance — and receive an answer from the computer almost immediately; but such a mode of operation in fact has not been practical with most first- and second-generation computers. It is only with the more recent computers that this on-line mode of operation has become feasible on a widespread basis.

What are the advantages of a fast response mode of operation?

1. Fast response systems can reduce human waiting time and the waste of human time — where humans must wait on the arrival of information before they can take action. In some cases, waiting is just annoying, but minimizing annoyance is a competitive factor. The airline reservation systems and savings bank systems are aimed at this problem. In other cases, an urgent situation exists — as in the case of law enforcement officers wanting information on a suspected stolen car. Also, fast response may be justified by facilitating executive decision making, it can provide executives the information needed while the decision is under study.

2. Fast response systems can reduce the idle time and waste of valuable resources. The utilization of limited equipment and machines can be improved, inventory safety stocks reduced, and money in bank accounts moved and put to work.

3. Fast response systems allow humans to handle more complex transactions within a "customary" waiting time. Public utilities are considering fast response systems to allow a customer service representative to determine what a customer's call is about — and handle it. The call might concern the customer's bill, request for new service, discontinuance of service — or an emergency repair call. The customer's call need not be referred to someone else; the representative can handle it on the spot.

4. Fast response systems keep information in step with fast moving external events. The stock quotation services must keep up with the stock market. Account balances must be determined quickly and accurately for authorizing credit sales, cashing checks, etc. Job shop production control must keep up with the many deviations from production plans that occur.

Examples of the competitive impact of fast response systems can be found in the cases of the airline reservation systems and savings bank teller systems. American Airlines introduced the first mechanized reservation system in 1948 (an electromechanical system in Boston) and an electronic computer system in New York in 1953. The service was so superior to the old manual methods that the other airlines were soon forced to install similar systems. American has continued to set the pace with the installation of a centralized system that keeps track of each passenger's complete itinerary, and other airlines are following suit.

Savings banks and savings and loan institutions have installed fast response systems for bringing a customer's passbook completely up to date while the customer is standing at the teller's window. All past unposted dividend or interest payments, as well as any unposted deposits, are entered automatically. These savings institutions report that, although previously they had often had forty to fifty people standing in line at dividend payment time, with the new systems they seldom had more than two or three people in line at each teller's window. In addition, a customer may go to any branch of the institution, not just one particular branch. The competitive pressure to adopt such a system is obvious.

We could continue this discussion for other areas. The point is, there *is* a place for fast response systems. When fast response is applicable, a company will either want to take the lead in installing a system or will have to respond later to such action taken by a competitor.

Data Communications. The fact that computers can communicate with each other will have many important ramifications in the business community. The use of data communications will not only reduce the time required for transmitting business data but it will also reduce duplication of effort and eliminate much manual effort.

Large grocery chains are already entering orders to food manufacturers through computer-to-computer communication. Of course, controls are built into the system to make sure that orders are not missed or duplicated. Stationery houses and hardware wholesalers have installed systems in which customers may enter orders by (a) dialing the phone number of the vendor's data processing system, (b) selecting a punched card that represents the item to be ordered and feeding it into a device attached to the telephone, and (c) entering the quantity requested via keys on the keyboard of the device. No written purchase order is transmitted. At the end of the month the stationery house or hardware firm provides each customer with a listing of all orders entered.

Eventually (and it may not be too far in the future) no written invoice will be prepared by such vendors; instead, invoices will be transmitted computer-to-computer, and not too long after that payment will not be made by a written check but by the transmission of payment data from the customer to his bank. Does all of this sound far-fetched and years away? At a major computer conference in Boston in early 1966 representatives of the American Bankers Association, a major computer manufacturer, a leading consulting firm, and the Telephone Company predicted that we would be witnessing in-practice examples of all of this by the early 1970's.

More Flexible Input and Output. Technological developments have made it easier to enter information into a computer and have provided faster, more convenient means for obtaining information from the computer. These developments offer substantial benefits and their use will grow.

One method employs the familiar teletypewriter which is connected either by teletypewriter line or telephone line to a computer, the choice depending on the economics and the number of users. When a user wants to enter data or enter an inquiry, he turns on the teletypewriter, waits for a go-ahead signal from the computer — within a second or so in well-designed systems — and starts typing in the information. If he makes an invalid entry, the computer prints out an error message immediately, on the same teletypewriter or on an adjoining one. Usually, the answer to an inquiry is printed out immediately after the inquiry message has been entered.

The Telephone Company has developed a simple Touch-Tone signaling device, which eventually will replace the dials on dial telephones; in the meantime, an auxiliary Touch-Tone device can be attached to any telephone. In fact, one variation is acoustically coupled to a telephone simply by putting the telephone handset into a special cradle attached to the Touch-Tone device. The user can enter numeric and some special character data from almost any telephone — but perhaps at the expense of interference to voice communications on the same cable. What are the possible uses? They are too numerous to list in detail. Salesmen can make their sales reports and enter sales orders — speeding up processing and eliminating much paperwork. Doctors and dentists can enter patient billing data. Credit authorization inquiries can be entered — with the answers supplied by the computer via simulated voice. The New York Stock Exchange is already answering inquiries from subscribers for stock information — latest price, high, low, volume, and so on.

Optical scanners have been developed to the point at which many typewritten business forms can be made suitable for scanner input, thus eliminating the key punching operation. The new scanners can read a variety of type sizes and fonts and can even read carbon copies. In fact, some scanners can read hand-printed numerals but scanners to read handwriting or to interpret the human voice probably will not be practical for some time. How can optical scanners be used? The Royal Crown Bottling Company in Los Angeles is having its salesmen take orders by marking optical scanner forms. The computer can then prepare lists showing the best loads and routes for the delivery trucks — as well as prepare customer invoices, which are printed on the same type of forms. If the customer wants more or less than was ordered, the delivery man simply marks the change on the form. Key punching is eliminated, paperwork is reduced, delivery costs have been halved. More generally, the economics of optical scanning compare very favorably with key punch costs where the volume will support it.

Display devices employing TV-like cathode ray tubes have been developed. They provide a faster means of displaying information from the computer because data can be presented more quickly on a CRT than it can be printed on a teletypewriter. In fact, the computer can transform numeric data into graphical form so that reports can be presented graphically. When a keyboard is coupled with such a device, a powerful means of man-machine communications is created. It will not be too long before large screen displays make their appearance for business uses, where the display is large enough for a group to observe. Such devices are already in use for military applications, but their cost is still somewhat high for commercial use. We discuss the impact of such devices in connection with the new management reporting systems.

These are only a few of the new technological developments that offer great promise, and we have covered only a few of their possible uses. They illustrate the point that data processing with the third generation of computers will be very different from data processing in the past. Although in their early stages of use, these developments are clearly beyond a speculative or theoretical stage.

Data processing management should be expected to see the benefits possible from such developments and to encourage projects aimed at making use of them. In addition, there are other developments that will arouse the interest of management — and competitive pressure is sure to develop for their adoption.

Pressure from Management

New Management Reporting Systems. Teletypewriters or CRT-display devices connected directly to the computer offer a new means of presenting management reports. True, they provide only a part of the mechanized management reporting system, but it is a valuable part. Also essential is the software (computer program) system for interpreting input data, retrieving necessary data from the files, processing the data and preparing reports, and presenting the reports on the teletypewriter or the CRT. Still another essential part is the data base itself (the totality of the data files), in which data must be stored in a consistent, easily retrievable manner.

What will these new reporting systems offer? Well, when an executive wants to find out something about the enterprise, he will not have to wait until the end of the week or the end of the month to find out. He (or an assistant) can enter the request on his personal console and get a report that is up-to-date as of, say, yesterday afternoon at close of business. Does this sound farfetched? Pilot systems are already in everyday use in exactly the manner described.

Let us consider an actual example; the company does not wish to be identified. A data file has been set up that holds details on potential sales, actual sales, expenses, and plans for both expenses and sales — for a portion of this company that covers a good part of the United States. The file is brought up-to-date every evening by the use of data communications. Each of the top dozen or so executives has his personal teletypewriter console, which sits beside his secretary's desk.

If an executive, who is authorized to receive this information, wants a report of sales versus planned sales for all districts for both month-to-date and year-to-date, he or his secretary enters his private code number and about a half line of typing to identify the desired report. The private code number does not print on the teletypewriter, because the keyboard and printer are separated, which helps to protect the secrecy of the number. Within a few seconds, usually, the report starts appearing. If he notes that one district is substantially below plan, he can call for a report on all sales offices within that district. If one or two sales offices account for most of the deviation, he can call for a report on actual sales versus expected sales for those offices. If sales have been lost to competitors, the competitors are identified in the file — and this can be reported in answer to further inquiry. With this probing ability — the ability to go down to the lowest level of detail when desired and in a few minutes — the executive can better identify the causes of trouble.

In fact, the executive can have the computer perform a sales analysis for him — trends in sales for his company and for competitors, when the information about competitors' sales is available. We have used this type of system in just such a manner — asking the computer to compute averages of selected transactions, compute trends, and detect major deviations. The interesting and surprising part of all this is that it takes only a few minutes of instruction and practice for a user to begin using such a system. True, the user's first efforts are slow and awkward, but even so he *is* using the system. It does not take days or weeks of training to get started.

The philosophy of this type of reporting system is that the executive gets only the information he wants when he wants it. If he wants a month-end report prepared without his asking for it and put on his desk by X day of the next month, fine — he can get it, and if by chance he wants to see this same report up-to-date in mid-month he can get that too. If he wants an unusual report that has not already been defined, he is provided with an easy means of asking for that report. He can probe for selected detailed data to as great a degree as the file will support.

We are touching only the high points of this new type of reporting system. There must be obvious safeguards in such a system — preventing unauthorized persons from obtaining the information, preventing unauthorized change of the data in the file, and so on. Workable solutions have been developed for all such problems that have come to light, and still more powerful solutions are known, though not yet implemented.

These reporting systems are in the very early stages of application. Still, as the benefits of such a reporting system become widely known, managements are sure to begin asking their data-processing people, "When will we have a system like that?"

The Corporate Data File. As mentioned just above, the data base itself will be an essential element of the reporting system. In order to support a management reporting system, the necessary data must not only be in the data base, it must also be stored in some consistent manner to be easily accessible. The term "data base" may sound esoteric at first, but we have come to find it a convenient term. It is short, easily remembered, and connotes the important concept that our information systems are built on a base of stored data. It does not mean anything fancy or mysterious; it just means the aggregate of the data in machine language available to the computer — inventory files, customer files, files of future plans, computer programs, and such.

Today, even though organizations using EDP often have huge amounts of data in machine language — on magnetic tape, in punched cards, or on magnetic disks — it is not uncommon for the managements of these organizations to find that they cannot get answers quickly to simple inquiries. The main reason is that the different data files have been set up in an inconsistent manner. Each file has been set up by a different programmer who is concentrating on the production requirements that the file must meet — the main output reports and other operating papers. Each file is custom designed. The different files may have different cut-off times or dates, so that the data in them cannot be easily compared. Or the data fields may be defined slightly differently. For instance, in two sales order files in the same company, but at different geographic locations, *gross sales* may have two different definitions: one may define it as "total sales" and the other as "total sales minus returns."

The solution to this problem of inconsistent data appears to lie in the direction of the *corporate data file* — a centrally controlled set of data definitions and formats. When a data file is set up, it must use the standard definitions of data fields, as well as standard formats such as the length of a field and location of decimal points, where blanks can occur. If new fields are needed, they must gain prior approval from the central staff before they become an official part of the corporate data file. The data itself might be geographically dispersed — each geographically separate EDP installation probably would have its own data files — but the data would be recorded in a consistent manner.

Other requirements for an effective corporate data file are data security provisions, an effective cataloguing system to direct the computer to any desired data, and provision for setting up temporary files that are not official parts of the corporate data file.

One of the benefits of the corporate data file will be that it will promote system integration. Applications can be more easily tied together if they use common data definitions. Geographically separated installations can be more easily consolidated. Of course, management inquiries can be answered much more quickly and effectively. Management's annoyance with inconsistent data is causing the pressure for the corporate data file to build up, and we expect that it will continue to build up.

We should mention that the creation of the corporate data file for an organization promises to be a large, difficult undertaking. From our study of the subject it appears to be much more difficult than, say, the conversion of a big application to the computer or the installation of an on-line system. We believe that it will be more than five years before many organizations will have made much progress toward this file, so it is an area in which management should not expect results too quickly. References to further discussion of the magnitude of this task will be found in the bibliography.

Computer-Assisted Corporate Planning. Computers will be playing an increasingly large role in corporate planning, by allowing management to test the consequences of alternative courses of action. Solutions can be tested in advance and the best alternative chosen. If unexpected events occur that require plans to be recast, the computer can help to reformulate the plans in a fraction of the time that manual methods require.

International Minerals and Chemical Corporation of Skokie, Illinois, has been making very interesting use of computer methods to aid corporate planning in recent years. IMC is a large producer of primary fertilizer ingredients — nitrogen, phosphate, and potash. They have developed a series of computer-based models for planning the production and distribution of phosphate.

The "world econometric model" considers the productive sources of phosphate in twenty-three countries throughout the world, as well as IMC's production locations in Florida and the western United States. Production at these locations interact with markets in more than forty countries. The model is used for simulating phosphate demand and production and the most probable world allocation patterns for the product.

For world distribution an "ocean transportation model" considers customer locations at forty-five ports in twenty-five countries, plus sixty-five more ports in which backhaul shipments might be picked up. This model is used for planning ten years into the future — during which time they foresee a 300 per cent increase in IMC's transportation requirements.

A third model is a more detailed representation of phosphate production in IMC's Florida mines. The model considers reserve positions and sales forecasts for five, ten, and fifteen years in the future, in an attempt to balance resources to sales for best profits. IMC can experiment with alternative forecasts and obtain successive production schedules, until the system is in balance.

A fourth model, a plant location model, is used for determining the scope and timetable for entering new markets. Part of the input for this model is output from the other models discussed.

IMC has been a most aggressive merchandiser in the fertilizer market, and the computer has played a significant role in their corporate planning activities. A good discussion of the company and their successful methods will be found in the March 1965 issue of *Fortune*.

The role of the computer in the planning function, as we see it, is to provide the following services:

- Analyze historical data, both internal and external to the company, to detect trends, opportunities and challenges.
- Project future eventualities, under different sets of assumptions,

through the use of models — again to detect opportunities and challenges.

- Analyze alternative solutions for selected opportunities and challenges by the use of models; determine costs and benefits.
- Aid in the development of detailed plans for selected projects, including schedules, cost estimates, and budgets.
- Aid in balancing resource use and in detailed cost control.

If for no other reason than competitive pressure, management will be forced to turn to the computer more and more to aid in planning activities during the next few years. The power of the computer is just being realized in this area.

Use of Management Science Techniques. At last, management science and operations research techniques are receiving the attention that was forecast for them some ten years ago. Now that many users of EDP have a large portion of their record-keeping operations converted to the computer, they are more willing to consider the introduction of mathematical methods to aid in decision making.

The most widespread use of mathematical methods to business has been in the area of inventory control. The military services spearheaded the development and introduction of these methods for their complex logistics systems. The techniques have spread rapidly to commercial use. A good discussion of the potentials of management science techniques, for application to business problems, will be found in another book of this series, *A Manager's Guide to Operations Research,* by Russell L. Ackoff and Patrick Rivett.

With the growing interest in the use of management science techniques, the need to analyze management information requirements will grow, and these management information requirements, in turn, tie in with the design of the corporate data file. We would expect to see projects set up in numerous companies to tackle this difficult area; up to now more lip service than actual support has been given to such studies.

Net Effect of These Pressures. We have listed some of the major developments — both in the technological area as well as the ways computers are being applied to management problems — that will catch the attention of both data processing management and executive management in the years ahead. The benefits that these developments promise are impressive. In the same way that most large organizations found it desirable to make use of a computer during the past decade we expect that most companies will want to take advantage of developments such as these in the next decade.

These new developments only compound the problem for data processing management, though. Data processing staffs are still confronted with the need to convert new record-keeping functions to the computer, make changes to existing programs, and consolidate existing applications to form more integrated systems. In addition, there will be a need to develop a series of computer programs to aid in the function of data processing planning itself, as we will discuss shortly. If additional projects are added for the types of developments just discussed, the project workload clearly becomes a deluge.

The net effect of these many projects, all crying for attention, is that project selection and scheduling becomes much more difficult than it has been in the past. Clerical savings, never a really good measure for project selection, becomes less and less a factor as these new areas are considered. "Experience" provides fewer guidelines for decision making because there is so little precedent to follow. Snap decisions and "quarterbacking" cannot begin to cope with the complexity of the problem. What is needed is a systematic means of project evaluation, selection, and scheduling for guiding the data processing program.

PLANNING FOR DATA PROCESSING

The elements of a systematic method for creating and maintaining plans for a data-processing program are:

1. Program direction and guidance; review list of challenges, opportunities, and problems to determine which should be evaluated first, in line with over-all company goals; coordinate data processing projects with other company projects.
2. Evaluate alternative solutions for the challenges, opportunities, and problems identified in Step 1 above; present results of evaluation to aid in project selection; select solutions and assign project priorities.
3. Determine "when and how" each project is to be performed and fit each such project into the over-all time schedule within the con-

straints of available resources; this over-all time schedule may cover over five years into the future.

4. Develop detailed plans and budgets for the next year, consistent with the long-range plans.

Before discussing this method, we should first define "challenges and opportunities." These are potential actions that will either solve an existing (or foreseen) problem or achieve a desired goal. As an example of a company that took advantage of an opportunity, consider the case of International Minerals and Chemical Corporation, mentioned above. IMC reasoned that they could sell more of their fertilizer products if they could give farmers good information on what would grow well in the coming season. So IMC developed a computer-based "water table model" — really an inventory of how much water is in the growing zone for many parts of the United States. Rainfall is added into the inventory; run-off and evaporation are subtracted from it. They advise farmers what to grow based on the water conditions. The model has been so successful that IMC has picked up substantial business from their competition.

The planning method does not involve going through the steps just once and in sequence. Rather some steps are performed in parallel, and a fair amount of iteration is required for creating a set of plans. Also, the planning process must be repeated from time to time, sometimes because of the occurrence of unexpected events that upset the previous plans.

Because each step is complex and must be repeated numerous times, the method is really practical only if most of the steps can be performed rapidly — for creating new plans and updating plans when important changes occur. So the method hinges on the degree of mechanization accomplished.

We discuss each of the elements of the method briefly.

Program Direction and Guidance. Many data processing installations appear to be directed by their "customers" — operating management requesting that certain jobs be done. In other cases the executive responsible for data processing directs the course; it is not unusual for strong animosities to exist between this man and some of his fellow executives who feel that he is "empire building."

We have been impressed by companies that have formed a top-level *steering committee* to guide and direct the over-all data processing program. One company that we talked to has the executive vice president as the chairman of the steering committee and other vice presidents as members of the committee. It may be a while before many companies will have data processing steering committees at this level, but as data processing becomes more of a competitive tool we believe that more companies will be able to justify the step.

The reason that a high-level steering committee is important is that it can evaluate the list of potential projects — projects aimed at the challenges, opportunities and problems — from an over-all company point of view. What we are saying is that data processing in the third generation of computers is a far cry from punched card tabulating. Data processing projects can and will affect the basic well-being of the organization — and they will deserve the same attention from executive management as do today's decisions on new products, new markets, methods of financing, and so on.

When a high-level steering committee is first formed, it is likely that it will not be too effective from a guidance standpoint. Data processing is still somewhat of a mystery to many executives and they may not be willing to take a strong stand on which projects would be best for the company. So in its early stages the steering committee may simply act in a judicial capacity — listening to the merits of various proposed projects and making a determination of priority. The committee can provide another valuable function at this time, that of protecting data processing management against pressure for sudden changes in plans. If someone in management suddenly gets excited about a new data processing possibility, of the kind we discussed earlier in this chapter, the committee should be able to assess the impact of this project on the data processing plans.

As the committee gains experience and confidence, hopefully it should give more guidance and direction to the program. What markets is the company aiming at and what level of performance is required to penetrate those markets? Can data processing aid in market penetration — by fast order entry or special customer services? How much of the data processing resources should be directed toward the corporate planning area?

Some people might argue that a committee is never a solution to a planning problem, that it is much better to assign responsibility to one or a few individuals. Committees *are* functioning effectively in the high management levels of many organizations today, for they provide a means of bringing the viewpoints of a number of executives to bear on a problem. As a general method of project selection applicable to a wide range of situations we favor the steering committee solution over the assignment of the responsibility to one individual.

What will the steering committee have to work with? The main material should be a list of challenges, opportunities, and problems related to data processing. This would be a list of possible projects, developed from the point of view of the whole organization, not just individual departments. So one function of the committee — one that they will have to delegate, no doubt — is to periodically or continually search for projects that should be considered. They should not just wait for proposals to come up the line from operating departments.

This process of searching for the challenges, opportunities, and problems is a basic ingredient of the planning process instituted in the Department of Defense in the early 1960's. We have listed some references to this planning system in the bibliography at the end of the book, for those who want to study the subject in more detail.

Evaluate Alternative Solutions. Once the relative importance of the challenges, opportunities, and problems has been established, the next step is to develop alternative solutions to each of them in turn and evaluate the cost and effectiveness of each solution. Here is a step in which the computer can be most useful.

The challenges, opportunities, and problems may be broader in scope than just data processing — they may involve the consideration of new products or new markets, in which the data processing function will play an important role — or they may be limited to an information processing area such as installing a fast response order-entry system. It is possible that the former situations will have been considered by, say, the corporate planning staff and passed on to the data processing steering committee along with suggested priorities.

Whatever the problem, someone has to conceive alternative

solutions. One of the key features of the "systems analysis" approach now being used by the Department of Defense is the exhaustive search that is made for alternative solutions. Normally we humans tend to grasp the first "good" solution we come across because our intuition tells us that we probably cannot find a much better solution and we might waste a lot of time looking for one. The "systems analysis" approach used by the military rejects this hypothesis; it says that an exhaustive search must be made.

We digress for a moment to explain the quote marks around "systems analysis." Here the term is meant to identify the highest level system studies of the types listed in Chapter 1. In data processing the term systems analysis has usually referred to the lower level studies. Eventually, perhaps it will have a less ambiguous meaning, as the level of the typical systems studies in data processing is raised.

Of course, the amount of time that can be spent searching for alternative solutions is a function of the size and importance of the problem. In some cases, only a few man-weeks can be justified in searching for the best solution to a problem. Also, good stereotyped solutions have been developed for some of the more routine operations; this is true, for example, for many batch-processed magnetic tape applications. When good stereotyped solutions exist, the search might concentrate on such questions as "can we perform this operation less frequently?" or "can we eliminate all or major parts of this operation?" rather than on the way the computer runs are organized.

In many of the larger computerized applications we have observed or participated in, however, we feel that the search for alternative solutions could have been much more exhaustive and to good advantage. This lack of an exhaustive search might be excused in years past on the basis of the existing state of the art, but this excuse is becoming less and less tenable. To illustrate, we worked on a number of retail customer-billing and accounts-receivable operations over a number of years in the early 1960's, each of which had essentially the same operating requirements. Over a period of some four years, *substantial* improvements were made in the system designs — and these designs were the solutions that we are talking about here. Computer operating times were cut to a fraction of their original amount — not only because the later computers were faster but also because the system designs were that much better. Possibly not all this improvement might have been realized by a more exhaustive search for alternative solutions at the outset, but certainly a good portion of it could have been realized.

The computer can play a role here, by aiding in the evaluation of possible solutions. One way in which the computer can perform this function is by *simulation,* in which a logical or mathematical model of the solution is processed by the computer. As an illustration, simulation has been used to develop improved work schedules for savings-bank tellers. A simulation model represents the random arrival of depositors and the various types of transactions they have — deposits, withdrawals, need to have passbook brought up to date, cashing of checks, etc. By testing different teller work schedules against these simulated arrivals of depositors (when the arrivals agree with the statistics of actual arrivals), improved work schedules can be selected. This same process can be used for simulating the arrival of transactions in a data processing system. The structure of the design (e.g., batch processing versus on-line processing, as two very different design structures), as well as the effect of changes in design parameters (the speed of the computer used or the number of magnetic tape units used), can be tested.

In Chapter 1 we talked about mechanized evaluations of alternative computer configurations when computer equipment is being selected. This type of program can be and has been used for testing the cost and effectiveness of different system designs. One evaluator system was used to design a large on-line system for the Department of Motor Vehicles of the State of California. With hundreds of remote terminals and large quantities of data to be stored (some 20 billion characters within the next few years), consideration of many alternative designs by manual means would have been impractical for this system.

We are describing what *should and can* be done, when studying the selected opportunities, challenges, and problems. For each such potential project, an exhaustive search should be made for alternative solutions. Each solution should then be evaluated in terms of its cost and its effectiveness. The best solutions to each problem, along with their costs and their effectiveness, can be presented to the data processing steering committee. The committee then makes the final selection of the projects to be worked on and the solutions to be used.

This concept is a goal toward which we believe EDP users should strive. The beginning steps can be made now, but it will be difficult to put a full-blown evaluation system into operation quickly. As we pointed out, simulation will play a big role in evaluating alternative solutions — but at the present time it is still fairly expensive to create a simulation model. Better simulation techniques are being developed rapidly and it is likely that the cost of creating a simulation model will be cut drastically. For instance, at the Rand Corporation in Santa Monica, California, they have developed a generalized simulation model of a job shop manufacturing plant. Any one of literally millions of specific models, to represent a specific situation, can be created in a few minutes time. This is done by filling in a questionnaire which provides data for control inputs to the model. Of course, the computer program is not the only big cost element; gathering the statistics about the system to be simulated is also a costly process. But we believe that the corporate data file will go a long way toward providing data and statistics quickly and economically, as users begin retaining more and more detailed transaction data in the corporate data file. The net result is that, while the use of simulation for evaluating alternative solutions might be restricted to only the larger, more important problems at this time — due to the expense involved — we see it being economically applied to a much broader range of problems before the end of this decade. Users should be working in this direction now.

Determining "When and How" of Each Project. The design and selection process is an iterative one. It is likely that during the evaluation step only preliminary designs will be used — designs that do not involve a high degree of detail. Of course, with mechanized evaluation techniques, greater degrees of detail can be considered than would be feasible if manual methods were used. If many alternative designs are being considered, it is logical that some degree of simplification and aggregation be used.

The evaluation results would be presented to the steering committee somewhat as follows: assume that a fast-response order-entry system, covering certain product lines of the company, was being considered. Several alternative system designs, those that showed up best of the many evaluated, might be submitted. One design might provide immediate input for any sales office at any time, with very rapid order checking, credit checking, inventory availability checking, and order acknowledgment. The effectiveness might be given a rating of 100, as far as customer service is concerned, and the cost would be indicated for conversion and operation. With another solution, using less central equipment, during times of peak use, a sales office might encounter a delay of up to, say, ten minutes before they could enter an order; the cost of this system probably would be less than the cost of the first solution. A third alternative might have even slower response at times and cost even less. In addition to the dollar costs, data such as the following should be supplied for each solution: requirements for systems analysis and programming time, personnel skill probably required versus skill available, and existing commitments on skilled personnel. The committee would have to consider the cost effectiveness of each solution, what performance that competitors are likely to offer the customers, the ability of the personnel to install a workable system, and so on. Armed with this information, the committee would then identify which solution looked best to them.

Having selected the solution, the next step is to find out in more detail how that solution would be implemented. More system design might be needed, with more detailed data. The major step at this point would be to work out a *time-and-action schedule* for developing and installing the solution. This is a one-time project — it is done once, not repetitively. Network techniques, such as PERT and CPM, have proved to be most effective for planning and controlling one-time projects. With the experience gained to date in these techniques, it is logical to assume that PERT, say, *would* be used for developing the time-and-action schedule for the project. (If PERT is not used, the manager making that decision should have a good reason for not doing so — not an answer that amounts to "Well, we tried it once but we like our old method better.")

We will not give a detailed description of PERT or CPM here; several excellent references are listed in the bibliography. Suffice it to say that these network methods start with a list of jobs that have to be done (the "activities") in order to accomplish the over-all project, along with time and resource requirements for each such activity. These activities are then arranged into a logical sequence

— a network diagram. Laying out the diagram and analysis of its implications can point out such things as the fact that the whole project cannot be completed as soon as desired, that some activities have been overlooked, or that more than the available resources are being committed during some time period.

The computer can play an important role in creating and maintaining such networks. Currently, the listing of the activities and the creation of the initial network diagram is usually done manually. This data is then fed into the computer which, using a network-evaluation program, computes the *critical path* (or paths) through the network — the paths that determine how long the over-all project will take. Advanced versions of PERT also estimate costs and resource usage. The person designing the network then usually has to make changes in an attempt to get the project done more rapidly and/or to level the use of resources. Then, as actual work occurs on the project, the activity completion times are fed into the computer and inserted instead of the estimated times. The computer recomputes the critical path and completion time, pointing out the need for possible corrective action. All of these steps are well within the state of the art.

We foresee the computer aiding in the development of the list of activities and creating the initial network diagram. This would require standard lists of activities, for different types of recurring projects; even though each project is only done once, its type is repeated. When a project is contemplated, a standard list of activities could be called up from storage and displayed on, say, a CRT console. The person designing the network could review the list and make any necessary changes for the particular project at hand — adding activities, deleting some, and changing estimated times. Once these changes had been made, the computer could draw the network and, if desired, present it on the CRT. Of course, the over-all network would be a summary network in order to be displayed on the CRT. The user could call for a detailed display of selected portions of the network.

The use of a network technique will point out, better than previous methods, the time schedule and resource utilization of the project. The next step is to fit this project into the over-all workload.

McKinsey & Company, management consultants, have developed

an interesting method for fitting projects into a schedule. Their method, by the use of a computer program, considers the costs and estimated savings for each project, as well as resource utilization, time period by time period. Given a set of projects, the program simulates "loading" the data processing staff; that is, it will assign projects in a time period up to the capacity of the staff to handle the projects. At the same time, it computes the net cash flow for each time period (considering the costs of the projects being worked on, and the expected savings from completed projects) and works out the present value of this cash flow. A number of possible schedules, along with the present value of each, are computed in this manner. The schedule with the highest present value would generally be the logical one to choose.

This method might be extended to projects that do not promise clerical-cost savings but instead promise, perhaps, higher sales through better customer service. Of course it is harder to attach a dollar value to such benefits, but an attempt must be made.

The end result of this processing is that project time-and-action schedules will have been worked out and these schedules will have been fitted into an over-all workload in a logical manner. This total workload may well extend five years or more into the future.

Develop Detailed Plans. Once the longer range plans have been laid out, as just discussed, the next step is to develop detailed plans and budgets for the next year.

The networks for the various projects will provide a good basis for developing the detailed plans. Subnetworks generally will be necessary, in order to break down the total project network; for example, the project network might have an activity that is named "study data processing activities of the order department." For detailed plans a network might be developed for this particular study, showing more specifically what is to be done when.

We have discussed networks in terms of estimating elapsed time and resource utilization; in PERT terminology, these are called PERT/TIME networks. The network concept has also been extended to the estimating and control of project costs through what is called PERT/COST. Intuitively it would seem that the cost of each activity could be estimated, and this would give a cost network — the approach originally tried. It proved to have too many problems (which are not discussed here), and it had to be simplified. Under PERT/COST, logical groups of work activities are identified and are called "work packages." In general, every activity must be a member of one and only one work package — but some things do not lend themselves to a nice clean assignment. Maintenance work is an example; it is hard to predict just what will need maintenance, or when. But the work-package concept is useful. Cost estimates are prepared for the work packages, and the costs are controlled by these packages.

So the time networks, developed in Step 3, provide a good basis for developing detailed work plans and budgets for, say, the next year. True, they do not cover such things as staff vacations, sickness, training of new employees, and other such factors that a department manager must consider, but they do cover the major consumption of resources in the data processing department. Moreover, these plans and budgets are tied to *why* the resources are being expended (the projects that have been selected by the data processing steering committee) as well as *how* they are being expended (salaries, machine rental, etc.).

What Action Can Be Taken Now?

It will be no small job to install a project selection and scheduling system of the type described in this chapter. Some organizations may feel that their data processing staffs are so heavily committed already that they cannot be diverted to "less pressing" work.

We suggest that most organizations *can* begin by *establishing a high-level data processing steering committee.* Early in its indoctrination, this committee can be appraised of the changing technology and the need for a systematic project selection and scheduling system. It is then up to the committee to find the best way to implement such a system.

Another thing that can be done immediately by most organizations is to *develop a comprehensive list of challenges, opportunities, and problems* that relate to data processing. Such a list is more than just the current backlog of projects. It should include projects that appear desirable because of competitive pressures — getting the jump on competition or responding to similar action by a competitor. At least once a year, this list should be brought up to date; it would be preferable to update it more frequently.

Another step that can be taken is to *start using methods that greatly increase the productivity of system analysts and programmers,* as such methods become available. Some, such as decision tables and decision-table translators, are available now. Others, such as generalized file-processing software systems, are in the late stages of development. These are described below. We mention them here because they may substantially increase staff productivity — on routine record-keeping conversions, at the least. Anything that will greatly increase the productivity of the data processing staff will help to reduce the backlog — and this in turn will tend to simplify project selection and scheduling.

3 Organizing the Effort

Data Processing's New Niche

If data processing is to undertake broader projects of considerable importance to an enterprise, its role in the enterprise must change. The effort must be organized so as to better support such projects.

As a case in point, the Department of Motor Vehicles (DMV) of the State of California, in Sacramento, is in the process of installing a large, advanced data processing system aimed at providing faster, better DMV services. Because of the significance of the project, the DMV created a new executive position, Assistant to the Director (EDP). This officer reports directly to the Director of the Department of Motor Vehicles and is the functional head of the departmental electronic data processing activities and advises the Director on EDP matters.

Why did the Director of Motor Vehicles move data processing management into his own office, by creating an assistant directorship? A brief review of the computer project will point up its significance to the department. The DMV has two major data files — the driver's license file and the vehicle registration file. With existing methods, applications for driver's licenses and license renewals are forwarded from the DMV field offices to Sacramento; the licenses are mailed to the drivers in two or three weeks. The same time schedule holds for the registration of new vehicles.

With the tremendous growth in the number of drivers and vehicles in California (a projected 50 per cent increase in the 1965 to 1975 decade), the DMV recognized that a major system improvement was called for, not just the computerization of existing procedures. So a fast response system is being installed; the initial equipment began arriving in mid-1966 and the target date for completing present plans is 1969. In this system DMV field offices will be connected to the computer complex in Sacramento by data communication lines and remote terminal devices, for fast response to inquires. Requests for driver's licenses and vehicle registrations can be processed more rapidly. Eventually it may be possible to issue a driver's license or vehicle registration while the applicant is waiting at the counter.

In addition to faster service for licenses and registrations, the DMV also wants to speed up the processing of inquiries. Currently the DMV receives some 15 million inquiries annually; by 1975 this number is expected to increase to 39 million. Such inquiries come from law enforcement agencies, other California departments, such as Justice, Public Works, and Public Health, the California courts, and commercial companies such as the National Auto Theft Bureau. About one fifth of these inquiries are urgent and will be handled in a minute or so by the fast response system.

It is evident that a system of this magnitude will fundamentally affect the way that the Department of Motor Vehicles will operate. It will change the whole main-line flow of information. It will substantially change many of the position descriptions, both in the Department at Sacramento as well as in the field offices. That is why the Department of Motor Vehicles has recognized data processing's new role.

This is only one example of many in which a project is so significant and can so profoundly affect the well-being of the organization that it has received its proper share of attention from executive management. This requirement for top management attention will increase and increase substantially. Executive management should and will want to be deeply involved in key decisions on new major system projects — such as a computer-assisted corporate planning system or a new management reporting system. These projects are too vital to the operation of the organization to be turned over to a lower level staff, with only infrequent progress reports to top management.

As the broader, more complex projects are undertaken, projects of the types we discussed in Chapter 2, data processing will take its place alongside marketing, production, finance, and engineering as one of the major functions of the enterprise. After all, the nervous system is a major subsystem of the body and the information system is a major function in the enterprise. As yet, this idea does not have wide acceptance; in many organizations, data processing is looked upon as simply "the old tabulating operation with chromium plating." We believe that this acceptance will grow rapidly in the next five to seven years, as the new data processing technology makes itself felt in the scope of the projects undertaken.

The Data Processing Executive

With data processing's responsibilities in these broader, more complex projects, the executive in charge of the data processing function will be dealing with the highest executive levels in the other functional areas. For example, a fast response order-entry system is of vital interest to the marketing function — and the vice president of marketing will want to be involved in key decisions during system design, as well as be kept up-to-date during critical conversion periods. The data processing executive must be in a position to deal effectively with this vice president on a person-to-person basis — and not have to work through two or three levels of management. The data processing executive should be a member of the data processing steering committe, and as we discussed in Chapter 2, this committe ought to include the upper executive levels. The data processing executive must be able to deal with men at the vice-presidential level, be able to argue his points with them, gain their respect. In short, he should be of the caliber of a second or third organizational-level executive.

At the same time we do not feel that the data processing executive's function can be adequately performed by the financial vice president. He has often perfomed this function in the past because data processing was located under the controller who might in turn have reported to the financial vice president. Data processing is becoming a complex, specialized area, and the financial vice president is a specialist in finance, not in data processing. When only routine record-keeping operations were involved, and financial record-keeping at that, this organization had some logic, but, as we have pointed out, data processing is bursting out of these bounds.

Of course, whichever executive currently has data processing located under him will resist losing "control" over this increasingly important function. He will probably interpret it as a loss of prestige, but keeping data processing under the financial function (or any other function, for that matter) is beginning to make as much sense as putting the engineering function under the financial vice president — or vice versa.

In the near future — the next three to five years — we foresee the data processing function reporting directly to one of the other functional vice presidents — most logically, perhaps, the vice president of administration, if such exists — in hundreds of organizations using EDP. Within ten years, we foresee the data processing executive himself at the vice-presidential level, for a good fraction of the using companies. While this may appear to be too sudden an organizational change, we believe that the rapid rate of change of the technology is going to force such action in the years that lie just ahead.

Looking at the problem from the other side, the chief data processing executive must have the respect of the people working under him — and this implies that he must have a good grounding in data processing. Data processing is a highly technical subject area that is growing more complex by the day. In the same way that the chief executive of the engineering function ought to be an engineer, the chief executive of data processing ought to have a good data-processing background.

All of this adds up to the point that EDP users ought to be planning to move data processing up at least to the third organizational level within the next three to five years and to the second organizational level within ten years. If the current manager of data processing is not of the caliber to meet these requirements, or cannot be developed to meet the requirements, it would be a good idea to start looking for the proper man.

ORGANIZING THE DATA PROCESSING DEPARTMENT

As background we review first the current EDP organizational forms. The major functions presently being performed in most data processing departments — not including managerial and secretarial functions — consist of the following.

System Analysis and System Design. In most installations one or more persons have been assigned the responsibility of working with line personnel in the study of an application to be mechanized. These people determine the requirements of the application and design the new system. They decide how many computer programs there will be, what data will be carried in the files, and so on. The logic of the program for each computer run is spelled out in sufficient detail so that programmers can work from it. Ideally, programmers should have to ask no questions on the logic of the program, such as "If such and such condition develops, what action should be taken?" Actually, what the system designer turns over to the programmers usually falls quite a bit short of this ideal. In fact, if the system designer *does* turn over a complete logical description, programmers object that their job is reduced to "just coding."

In the higher level system studies system analysis and system design can become quite complex. System analysis may involve determining requirements for a completely new system, in which there is little precedent to go on. System design may involve the creation of mathematical or simulation models for testing alternative designs.

System analysts must know the principles of data gathering (what data to gather about the present system). As part of system design, they must understand clerical procedures, forms design, computer-run design, file design, data communications, operations of a data processing installation, use of remote terminals, and programming.

Applications Programming and Program Maintenance. Applications programmers translate the program-run logic and file designs into the detailed instructions required by the computer. They debug programs and related groups of programs, and should document the programs to facilitate future changes. When given the logical description of changes to programs, they insert these changes. (This is *really* an iceberg statement; changing a program is sometimes more difficult than writing the original program, because the effects of a change can spread out like ripples on water.) Program maintenance is often considered degrading work — programmers like to work on new projects — but it may require a good part of the programming staff's time.

In some installations system analysts do the programming; in others the two functions are separate. When the two functions are combined, a higher level programming language, such as COBOL, is often used. When the two functions are separated, the programmers may prefer to work with a more detailed language, such as Autocoder.

Operations. The operations function has several components. One obviously is the operation of the computer and its peripheral devices, such as the high-speed printer, card reader, and tape units. This function is the highest level of the operating functions; one common source of supply of personnel has been programmers who would rather push buttons than push pencils.

Operations also include the key-punch and verification functions, as well as (at many installations) the control group. The control group logs in batches of incoming transactions, records or develops control totals and checks on reports coming out of the computer room, and perhaps distributes the copies of the reports to the distribution lists. Operations also include the function of records storage, performed by a person sometimes called the "tape librarian." All magnetic tapes must be correctly and clearly marked and stored in designated positions in the tape storage room, so that they may be accurately and quickly retrieved.

Development of New Methods, Software, and Equipment Selection. This complex area deserves a lengthy discussion. We treat it only briefly here and go into more detail in Chapter 5. New methodology and software can be developed internally or procured from other sources; new equipment is normally obtained from outside sources. If methods and software are to be developed internally, skilled personnel are required — and normally must be assigned to this function. In a great number of installations this function is *not* a clearly assigned responsibility.

When methods, software, and equipment are obtained from outside sources — as is normally the case — skilled people are needed to evaluate the alternative offerings and recommend courses of action. Here is a function that must be performed *frequently* by all users of computers. But often it too is handled in an informal fashion — often by assigning whatever applications programmer happens to be free at the time when an assignment must be made.

Here, then, are important functions that must be performed in almost every EDP installation, but they are not well handled and they are not recognized by most data processing departments in their organization charts.

Data Processing Planning. This function includes conceiving, developing, and proposing projects and the scheduling of selected projects to meet priority assignments and available resources. These tasks are often performed by the manager of data processing. He also creates the departmental budgets. The function includes equipment selection, but this task is usually reassigned to one or more of the programmers or system analysts, as already discussed. The function also includes analysis of alternative means of financing new equipment — whether by renting, leasing, installment purchase, or outright purchase. In the past renting equipment from the computer manufacturer has been favored about three fourths of the time. With the third-generation equipment, which promises a longer useful life, both long-term leasing and outright purchase are being given greater consideration.

Training. The data processing department is often called on to give as well as to receive frequent instruction. The department offers executive training courses or seminars to acquaint management with computer concepts. Personnel in line departments must be trained in the use of a new system during the early stages of conversion. Data processing personnel must go to school to learn about new equipment and programming languages. As in some of the other functions, this training is usually not assigned to specific personnel except perhaps in the large organizations. Instead, almost any member of the programming or systems staff may be called on from time to time to do the instructing.

These, then, are the major functions that must currently be performed in most data processing installations. Seldom are all of them recognized by the department organization; the most typical is to have the department divided into two or three sections — system analysis, programming, and operations.

Next we consider how these functions are being changed by the new technology and the probable impact of these changes on future departmental organization.

The Effect of Emerging Technology on Data Processing Organization

If we examine the trends of the system analysis and programming technology over the past decade, we find that more and more of the functions are being transferred to the computer. In the mid-1950's, the steps of problem definition, design of the system, detailed logic specifications, and translation to machine language were all done manually. With the arrival of compilers, the last of these steps became mechanized. A programmer could write programs in a language more suitable for humans, and the compilers would translate to the machine language. With the arrival of decision tables (which we will discuss in more detail in Chapter 5), a system analyst can describe the computer-program logic in tabular form; in addition, programs are available which can translate the tables into the application programs. With the arrival of flexible application packages (also to be discussed in Chapter 5), the boundary is pushed still further back, well into the area of system design. There is no reason to believe that this trend will stop in the near future; we expect it to continue.

System Analysis and System Design. Two major changes are occurring that will affect the role of the system analyst and system designer. One change was described in the paragraph above, where many of the routine aspects of systems work are being transferred to the computer. With the arrival of flexible application packages, much of the traditional work of the system analyst will vanish. True, *someone* has to do the system analysis and design — but once done, their work can be used by a large number of organizations.

The other change is the movement toward broader systems and the introduction of the new technology. Application packages in the past have trailed the technology — which means that the suppliers of the packages had to solve a large number of specific problems before they could generalize the solutions into the final applications packages. So the systems people will be moving in the direction of the more challenging projects at the same time that applications packages will be used for the more routine projects.

One direction is toward more extensive use of operations research. It is not likely that today's systems people will be able to perform operations-research work; in general, they do not have the mathematical background for it. But we foresee them working closely with the O.R. people, in developing new systems. A leading O.R. consultant told us that, of the projects he has worked on, he estimates that about 10 per cent of the man-hours expended were by O.R. people and 90 per cent were EDP-system analyst man-hours.

It is very possible, of course, that the operations research analysts will become the senior system analysts in the future. The broader, more sophisticated projects that will be undertaken may well call for their talents, more than have the routine projects of the past. But for the next few years at least, we exepect to see two staffs — one for system analysis and design, and one for operations research. The two will have to work quite closely on some projects.

Applications Programming and Program Maintenance. As already mentioned in connection with the changing technology, more and more of the functions of the applications programmer are being transferred to the computer. We expect this trend to continue to the point where the role of the applications programmer (as we know it today) is practically eliminated. As the programming function becomes more mechanized, speed of getting new applications on the computer will be increased. Similarly, program maintenance will be eased. We discuss the potential of generalized file processing software and decision tables to accomplish these benefits in Chapter 5.

What will happen to the applications programmer? Like the system analyst, we see him moving into more challenging areas. For one thing, someone has to write the general-purpose software — the software that is used to replace the applications programmer in user organizations. Someone has to modify this software and keep it current. Then, too, a need is becoming recognized for *data specialists* who organize and design the data files, make sure data definitions are correct and consistent, etc. The corporate data file of the future demands consistent data definitions; today, each programmer defines his data file pretty much as he sees fit. With the corporate data file, the applications-oriented person — the systems man — will have very little to say about *how* the data is stored in the system. And the systems man will have much less freedom in defining the contents of data fields, or in establishing new data fields. Instead these functions will be performed by the data specialist.

There will be work aplenty for machine specialists in the installations of tomorrow. But it will not be applications programming, as we know it today.

Operations. Operations will be greatly affected in the future. With the increased use of remote terminal devices, for capturing data at the source, as well as with the use of optical scanning, the need for key punching and verification will decrease. Controls will be built into the mechanized systems, and there will be less call for a group that records and checks control totals for batches of data. More and more of the data will be stored on-line to the computer (an advance made possible by the improved economics of mass storage devices) thus reducing the need for the tape librarian and for machine operators to mount and dismount magnetic tapes. With the use of remote terminal devices, there will be less need for entering data into the computer via cards, or extracting data from the computer via the high-speed printer.

These changes in operations, though, may not occur quite as quickly as the change in applications programming, in our opinion. The economics of remote terminal devices as yet are not such that they are expected to take over the bulk of the input operation by, say, 1970. Magnetic tapes are still the most economical form of bulk data storage; with expected improvements, they may well remain so for a number of years. So at least some of an installation's data may remain on tape, with the consequent need for tape library facilities as well as the mounting and dismounting of tapes on tape units.

The machine operator probably will have to be more skilled than today's console operator. Today, computers are used mostly in the batch mode of operation — the computer works on the jobs sequentially, one job at a time. If an error occurs, the operator knows which job has caused it and has an established procedure for restarting the job. But when the computer is working on several jobs concurrently — a few milliseconds at a time on each one — and if some errors are transitory (such as mistiming in a mechanism in a mass storage device), then the console operator has a real job cut out for him. We would expect *this* change in operations to show up in the near future, as computers are used in a multiprogramming (multiple jobs concurrently) mode of operation.

Development of New Methods, Software, and Equipment Selection. As the back-breaking load of applications programming is removed from an installation, it would be hoped that more effort could be devoted to this "research" aspect of data processing. Skilled programmers might develop software to meet the installation's needs, or develop improvements to existing software. System analysts might develop better methods for their functions — or at least try out new methods that others have developed.

Using organizations may find it hard to retain skilled programmers and machine specialists. Even now many of them are being lured to the new software companies. We will discuss this point more in the next chapter. But we want to point out here that this loss of an installation's best machine-oriented specialists may require that this "research" function be purchased from outside the company. In other words, an installation may have to buy this service from one of the software or consulting firms.

Data Processing Planning. We would hope that this function will develop along the lines discussed in the last chapter. From that discussion, it is apparent that the function is large enough and important enough so that it should be officially recognized as a separate function on the organization chart of the department. Management-oriented information-system designers should staff it.

Training. It appears that the training function performed by the data processing department will increase, before it ultimately diminishes. The third generation of computers brings with it more complex equipment, broader uses of the computer, and new concepts. Training for executives and line personnel in these new ideas is probably something that cannot be turned over *in toto* to the regular training department. The training department can aid in developing the needed training, but the technical knowhow must come from the data processing specialists.

The arrival of the new equipment also means more training for the data processing staff, for learning to use and operate the equipment. System designers must learn in some detail the characteristics of newly available equipment, so they can determine whether they have applications for it or not.

To complicate the picture somewhat, *computer-assisted instruction* is arriving on the scene. This is an instructional approach similar to "programmed instruction," originally developed by Dr. B. F. Skinner of Harvard. But instead of the material being presented to the student via printing on paper or via projection from a film, the material is presented to the student via a remote terminal (preferably a CRT-type terminal, for speed of operation). The computer presents the material, asks the questions, checks the answers, and keeps detailed records on how each student is doing. If a student is doing poorly in an area, the computer may start giving him more tutorial material or will signal the human instructor that the student needs help. Because of the power of the computer in this role, it is likely that at least the larger organizations will start using it as a part of their regular employee training methodology. And who may have to help the training department develop computer-assisted instructional material? Very possibly the data processing staff, unless the desired material can be obtained from outside sources. Here is another training function that may have to be added to the workload.

Organizing the Department

What do these trends in the technology add up to? How should the data processing function be organized in the years immediately ahead?

The field is entering a period of rapid change, even more rapid than it has been accustomed to. Precedent is either limited or does not exist, so it is not possible to give firm guidelines on how best to organize data processing. The following are suggestions for consideration more than they are guidelines.

The function should be headed by a man at least capable of operating at the third organizational level — that is, reporting to a vice president. While it may not be desirable in a particular case to move data processing up to this level immediately, plans should be laid for doing so within the next two or three years, in our opinion. The head of the function should be of the caliber required at this level and should have an appropriate title. "Director of Information Services" is currently becoming popular because "Manager of Data Processing" is too closely associated with a fourth- or fifth-level organizational unit.

If it has not already been done, the various data processing functions we have listed and discussed should be brought under this executive. One possible exception is the control group. From an internal control standpoint, the control group might be organizationally separate; auditors should be checked for their views on this point. As a digression, the electronic computer is the greatest potential tool for an embezzler so far created. As we write this, no large embezzlement involving a computer has been detected. We are constantly amazed how casual most companies seem to be on this point. Apparently it is going to take a large embezzlement to shake up managements and make them aware of the risks here.

It would be wise to expect that the organization chart for the data processing function will change in the next few years. Applications programming hopefully will diminish, if the new techniques perform as well as they are appearing to, and if users will use them. Management sciences will appear, if they have not already done so, and probably will be organizationally separate from system analysis and design. The operations researchers would want it separate from data processing — on as high or on an even higher organizational level. But this is not the place to argue this particular point, rather just to acknowledge that it exists. Operations may gradually diminish in the number of people required, particularly in key-punching, verification, and control. The job requirements for console operators will increase, as the equipment gets more complex.

Key positions in the department probably should not be staffed by highly machine-oriented personnel — such as are the applications programmers in most of today's installations. The trend is toward developing methods so that the user can define his needs directly for the machine, even if at some sacrifice in machine efficiency. For a while at least, systems people will be intermediaries between users and the computer, even after the applications programmer has been removed from the main line. But eventually even the role of the systems man will be affected, as he is bypassed by the user who communicates directly with the machine. The evidence that we have seen indicates that the thinking of the machine-oriented specialist too often is counter to this trend. Such a person often tends to hold to the old method — brute-force programming with "assembly level" programming languages (such as Autocoder, Easycoder, and Neat). Such a person in a key position in data processing could seriously hamper a company's progress along the lines we have been discussing in this book. That person's arguments may sound realistic, practical, and unassailable at the time he makes them — but the company will wake up to find that its competitors have passed it by.

ORGANIZING DATA PROCESSING PROJECTS

There are a variety of ways in which staff have been organized for data processing projects. We will discuss four of the more common approaches.

Project Headed by Systems Staff. This seems to be the most common form of project direction, from what we have observed. The systems staff of the data processing department conceives the project, sells it to line management, and then takes responsibility for implementing it. The line department(s) may or may not assign full-time persons to the project; usually, though, at least a part-time liaison person is assigned — an assistant manager or key supervisor who knows the department's operation well.

Those favoring this approach claim that the creative work must be done by the system specialists, and that if the operation is to be implemented well, the system specialists must control the project. The major problem is that the system specialists cannot make the new system work. Only the line personnel can do that, because they operate the system. If tension exists betwen the system staff and the line personnel, then the line personnel resist making the new system work, preferring to fall back on the old system. And the less the line personnel participate in the planning and implementation of the new system, the more chance there is for misunderstanding. Misunderstanding breeds tension and hence resistance.

Project Headed by System Staff with Heavy Participation by Line Personnel. We participated in one advanced project where the personnel consisted of four to five people representing a central systems staff, plus a number of people from the line departments. Most of the line personnel participated on a part-time basis, but from time to time were spending most of their time on it. A few line personnel were fully assigned to the project. The approach was effective in stimulating the enthusiasm of the line personnel, for they were aware of what was happening at every stage.

The major problem of such an approach is that the line personnel are on "detached service" when participating on the project. That is, they are working under a supervisor who cannot give them raises or promotions. Even worse, their regular supervisors who can give them these things do not have a chance to review their work. If the project is a lengthy one, they may feel that they are being passed by when promotions and raises are considered. Also, they may not be as compatible with their temporary supervisor as they are with their regular ones.

Project Headed by a Line Manager. The project may be conceived by a line department or line management may feel that it is so important that they must retain control of it. In this case both line personnel and system specialists are usually assigned full time to the project — and it is the system personnel who are now on "detached service." The same criticisms of detached service apply here. In addition, the system personnel feel that the critical design decisions are made by line personnel who are not fully trained in systems concepts.

There can be the danger that the line manager responsible for the project will be autocratic. Being a line manager, perhaps he can get away with this attitude better than a staff person in charge of a project, but autocratic methods breed resentment, which in turn causes resistance.

Project Headed by Line Manager, in Partnership with the Systems Staff. This project organization is somewhat similar to the preceding one except that the line personnel work under the line manager and the systems staff works under data processing management. The relationship between the two groups is a true partnership — neither can be an autocratic boss. The line manager heading the project is like the senior partner in a large partnership.

Although this form of project organization may sound ungainly and hard to control, it works suprisingly well in the situations we have seen. In fact, in the general case we would judge it to be the most effective of the project organizations with which we are familiar. The line manager is made responsible for the success of the project — he must *make* it work. He in turn can ensure the participation of other key line personnel. He cannot dictate to the system staff; he has to work problems out with them just as one partner does with another.

A Suggested Organization for Projects

Even though most data processing projects have been conceived by and run by the data processing system staffs, we do not favor this approach, particularly in the years just ahead. Projects are getting broader and more complex. The new systems that are being installed deviate more and more from the existing systems. Line managements, who are ultimately responsible for operating the new systems, will be more and more apprehensive about the workability and reliability of these new systems. The best solution to this problem with which we are familiar consists of three parts:

- Heavy participation by the affected line departments.
- Project leadership by a key line manager.
- A partnership relationship between line personnel and system specialists.

Participation by line personnel in a study of the present system and the development of a list of requirements that the new system must meet usually pose no problem. These people simply form part of the data gathering team — collecting samples of reports and forms currently in use, decision rules for handling a variety of transactions and so on. The problem is how to have them participate effectively during the design stages of the new project.

We have had rather consistent success with a technique which we call *design sessions,* for the solution of this problem. In the design session approach, a small group of people (six to eight, preferably) representing both line management and the system staff, devote essentially full time for up to several weeks to sketching out the preliminary design of the new system. Following this, the line managers are usually willing (nay, happy) to turn the preliminary design over to the system staff for filling in the details. Of course, it takes high-level management approval in order to take a number of good managers away from their jobs for days or weeks. But the key to success is to get these men thinking about the new system, and not about the problems currently on their desk.

The question might come up: do not the line managers have to have a deep understanding of computers in order to participate? The answer is no. They are in the design sessions to determine just what they want the new system to do, which functions to include in the new system and which to exclude (at least at first). The system staff representatives can indicate what is feasible technologically and what is not, during the design sessions. Also, the system staff can challenge the managers if their thinking tends to be too restricted or concerned with petty details. For instance,

"Why are we trying to cut customer order processing time from four days to three days? Why don't we consider cutting it to fifteen minutes, and see how that would benefit the company?" If a drastic improvement is desired, the managers can no longer think in terms of minor changes to current methods.

In addition to heavy participation in the project by line personnel, we believe that line management should be assigned the specific responsibility for the success of the project — and to us, this means that a line manager should be the project leader. There are several requirements that this line manager should meet, based on instances we have seen. He should be of a positive frame of mind, not a critic — but yet he has to anticipate troubles. He must want to see an improved system, rather than prefer to see the status quo maintained. He should be willing to work with the data processing people on the partnership basis. He must not be so enamored with the glamor of the computer that he forgets that his biggest problems will be "people problems" — training people in the new system, thrashing out expected problems with the line managers who are beginning to panic at the thought of the new system, etc.

The question of organization — to whom the data processing function reports, how it is organized, and how projects are organized — will become even more important with the arrival of the third generation of computers. As the data processing projects become broader, more complex, and more basic to the health of the enterprise, organization must change to reflect this situation. This is a question upon which action can be taken now, as we have pointed out — and it is a question that deserves attention by the highest levels of enterprise management.

4 Staffing the Operation

The questions uppermost in the minds of data processing management when staff requirements for future, more complex projects are considered, are the following:

- Is our current staff capable of handling these more complex projects?
- If not, how do we best obtain the necessary capabilities?

We discuss these two questions primarily in terms of system analysts and programmers, for they are likely to be the most limited of personnel resources in the years just ahead. We have a few comments to make on management science personnel.

Why are programmers being discussed if (as we stated earlier) the application programmer is likely to be phased out? This phaseout will not happen overnight; there is a big impetus behind machine-language programming. Even higher level programming languages such as COBOL and PL/1 do not eliminate the need for the programmer. The generalized file processing software systems and other developments that promise to reduce the role of the applications programmer are still under development; their breadth of application has yet to be determined. It is not yet apparent to what degree these new techniques will apply to on-line systems, for instance. So, although we foresee a reduction in the role of applications programming, it is not going to be eliminated in the next five years. Hence the need to consider sources of supply of applications programmers.

Is Our Current Staff Capable?

This is obviously a question to which we cannot give a general answer. It depends upon what a specific company requires of its staff, as well as that staff's particular capabilities *through time —*

since skilled data processing people have a habit of moving on to other jobs.

What are the characteristics of these future, more complex projects that will make them challenging to current staff members? Here are some of their likely technical aspects:

1. With on-line systems, programs must often operate within severe time constraints and also within computer memory constraints; data must be protected from damage or tampering; the system reliability requirements may be severe because when the system is down, everyone will know it.

2. With data communications systems, the different remote terminals often will have different transmission rates, data codes, and control codes; errors must be detected and handled without a loss of data, if possible; message routing can be complicated, including multiple destinations in store-and-forward systems and the need to recover messages previously transmitted.

3. File design will be more complex and must meet not only "production" requirements but also the need to answer complex inquiries rapidly; file size may be huge, measured in tens or even hundreds of *billions* of characters for even medium-sized organizations; file growth will be irregular and must be accommodated without reprogramming.

4. Management science techniques will be more widely used, including the use of simulation, linear programming, and general purpose statistical techniques; staff members must be able to work with operations research people on projects where such techniques are used.

5. Other technically complex areas with which the staff must become conversant include multiprogramming and multiprocessing, use of remote consoles, use of optical scanning, use of time-sharing, and data retrieval indexing techniques.

In this list we are able only to hint at the degree of complexity involved. The point is that the great majority of today's installations have had no exposure to any of these areas of complexity — or at most they have been exposed to perhaps one of the areas. They do not have the background for these areas, but future systems will involve most of all of them.

Moreover, the complexities represented by these several areas are much greater and more difficult to master than has been true in the past. In the past, it has been possible and practical to select a young person with a high I.Q. (since programming aptitude tests are really intelligence tests), give him a short training course in programming, and put him to work. A few such people have performed brilliantly, the bulk have performed adequately, and a few have dropped out. Although the problems they have worked on — generally batch processing of routine applications — may have been difficult to program, they have not had the inherent complexities of these future projects. So we cannot assume that because a person has performed adequately on batch-processed applications he will perform satisfactorily on these more complex projects.

Perhaps a key to the answer to the question — how good is our present staff — can be found in the efforts of the present staff to upgrade itself. The field has been dynamic from its inception, with new developments occurring continually. What has the current staff done to keep abreast of these developments?

Following are some generalizations about system analysts and programmers that we have drawn from the literature and from our experiences in the field. These generalizations might help to answer the question — how good is our present staff — in the "typical" installation. We describe what we believe to be the most typical case, recognizing that there can be sizable variations from this average.

System Analysts. In business data processing installations the system analysts may or may not be college graduates. The majority, based on the statistics we have seen to date, has had some college training. Whether they are college graduates or whether they have had college training, as far as we have observed, often has not been an important factor in job performance for batch-type processing of record-keeping functions. Even the college graduates, however, have had little or no mathematics beyond algebra; the odds are they will never develop sufficient mathematical sophistication to do creative management sciences work. Generally, system analysts have worked for their employers for a number of years and are quite well acquainted with application areas, such as production control or inventory control. Although they know the current procedures for these applications, they generally are not searching for substantial simplifications or performance improvements; instead they are concerned more with minor improvements. They have had little or no programming experience and do not appear to desire it. Only a fraction of the system analysts are sufficiently concerned about self-improvement to attend professional meetings on their own time. They are very practical-minded and are interested mainly in hearing about new techniques that they can apply rather soon to their work assignments. They have some company loyalty but recognize that EDP system analysis experience is at a premium and that they can probably change jobs readily.

Programmers. In business data processing installations, the programmers are usually younger than the system analysts. They may be newly hired people who did well on the programmer aptitude tests, or college graduates who have been hired into the position. Their experience with the company is usually fairly limited, and their knowledge of company operations is normally restricted to the programs they have worked on. Seldom does a programmer know a total application, except in those installations where they have had to double as system analysts. In general, programmers make less effort toward self-education than do system analysts; possibly this is because their workload is heavy and constant, and they want to forget about work in the evening. They have little company loyalty, because they know that their experience is valuable elsewhere and they see little opportunity for progressing up the management ladder in their company. Their programming knowledge is fairly limited, and is based upon an application of what they learned in one or two short programming courses plus job experience. Generally they are not able to analyze or modify software.

Of course, there *are* good computer people in user organizations. But when they gain experience, they frequently leave. The independent software companies are attracting a good share of the skilled people, as we will discuss shortly.

All in all, we feel that data processing management should not feel complacent about the staff problem. It has been bad enough in the past, and we think that it is going to get worse. At the very least, management should be thinking and taking steps to give current staff members additional training in preparation for the more complex jobs ahead. Management should also seek ways of making

clear the advancement opportunities open to analysts and programmers.

SOURCES OF CAPABLE PERSONNEL

If an organization's present staff is likely to have trouble with the
upcoming complex projects, and if present staffing methods are inadequate to meet the situation, what can be done? We see the
following ways for adding to staff, each of which should be
analyzed:

- Training your own staff, including both upgrading of existing staff
  and the selection of novices for apprentice-type training.
- Hiring trained people from the outside, including both people with
  prior data processing experience as well as people with college
  training in data processing.
- Buying outside services, including the use of the independent software firms and the use of consultants.

We discuss each of these sources of supply in more detail to
determine which are the most likely to be successful.

Training Your Own Staff

The approach of selecting people who already work for a company
to take computer training has been the one most widely used in
business data processing. It certainly will be given first consideration as a means of obtaining the necessary personnel in the next
few years. There are two aspects to consider: upgrading the existing
staff, and the selection and training of novices. We will consider
each in turn.

Upgrading Existing Staff. Experienced data processing people
ought to be able to be upgraded to meet the more demanding requirements of future projects. The upgrading can be accomplished
by means of special courses, as well as by some on-the-job experience.

The advantages of staffing by this method are evident. Management knows the people and knows what it can expect from them
— or perhaps more importantly, what it should not expect from
them. These people are more familiar with the business. They
ought to be anxious to receive the training because it will increase

their professional capability. Also, such training *should* increase their company loyalty — but there is no guarantee that it will.

On this last point, some organizations such as the Federal Government have resorted to employee contracts to protect themselves. That is, if the employee is to be given a valuable education or training at the organization's expense, he must first sign a contract that he will stay with the organization for a designated period after the training. If he does leave before the designated period has elapsed, he must reimburse the organization according to a schedule specified in the contract.

There are, of course, a number of shortcomings to this method of staffing. Firstly, few special courses exist to meet the requirements, and often those that do exist are lacking in depth. While the computer manufacturers offer a variety of courses, almost without exception these courses have covered only what the manufacturer thinks the user should know — which is "how to use *our* equipment and software." Little or no training has been given in system analysis techniques, system design methods, principles for designing and writing software, and so on. Also, obviously, such courses seldom point out the shortcomings in the manufacturer's products. Nor do such courses cover (in general) anything offered by another manufacturer — certainly not of a competitive manufacturer. We expect that these same features of manufacturer's courses will continue to exist.

Software companies are beginning to offer courses, and it is to be hoped that they will be more appropriate to the user's needs. Certainly, a software company should be objective on the subject of equipment and manufacturer-supplied software. But these companies might be expected to be biased on the subject of their own proprietary software. To date this proprietary software has not been much of a factor in affecting such courses, but it may become more of a factor in the future.

Universities and colleges offer a variety of evening courses and special one- or two-week seminars on computer subjects. But these courses seem to lag the technology. We have received a large number of such course announcements and somehow they have not seemed to fit the needs for upgrading current staff members in data processing system design, analysis methods, equipment-selection methods, software design and implementation, or such. Many of these courses are aimed at the engineering and scientific members of the computer field; while some of the principles might apply to business data processing, the language of the courses is not appropriate for business-oriented people.

Perhaps the needed courses *will* be developed to aid in upgrading existing staff members. The opportunities certainly exist. At present it is not certain that they will develop in time. We have a number of suggestions on what an organization can do to remedy this situation, which we discuss shortly.

Much the same problems will exist with on-the-job training — because it is likely to deteriorate to trial-and-error training. If no one in the organization understands the new techniques and if there are no courses to train the people properly, then the staff will only be able to plunge ahead and hope that things work out well.

Another shortcoming of this method of staffing is its likely impact on salary schedules. As the staff members become more proficient in advanced techniques, they will expect higher salaries. If the organization does not raise their salaries, they will begin looking for other jobs. With the shortage of trained people, it is to be expected that they will find other jobs. So, although data processing salaries already pose a problem in equitable salary administration, the situation is likely to get worse.

While the upgrading of existing staff will be widely used for meeting future staff requirements, we expect that organizations will have to supplement this approach with others. It appears to us that it cannot be depended on as much as has been the case in recent years.

Selection and Training of Novices. Another major source of personnel for business data processing has been the selection of (usually young) people from within the organization and giving them some computer training. Programmer aptitude tests have been a key selection device used by many organizations; test scores are supplemented by checking work experience and by personal interviews. When novices from outside the organization are hired for data processing, the same procedure is used except that references must be checked. If such people are just graduating from college, they may have no useful references from a work-habit standpoint. These novices are given a computer course—most often a one- or

two-week programming course presented by the computer manufacturer — and then put to work. Their first assignments are usually
not too demanding; in essence, they receive on-the-job training
for a period of about six months.

This method has been successful in a number of instances of
bringing young, talented people into many data processing departments at reasonable salary levels. In our experience, such people
tend to become more machine-oriented than business-oriented —
but this probably is because their first assignments have been
programming ones.

There are some shortcomings to this method. The major programmer's aptitude tests have become badly compromised. People
have often taken one major test six or seven times. We are told
that it is not unusual for college fraternities to have copies of the
latest aptitude tests in their files. Also, even if the aptitude tests
were not compromised, their results have not always correlated
too well with job performance. Using supervisors' ratings as a
measure of job performance (not a completely satisfactory measure,
to be sure, but the best that is currently available), aptitude test
scores correlate about 0.1 to 0.4 with these supervisors' ratings.
Some statisticians are quite dubious of correlations below 0.7 of
having any useful meaning — but if this severe criterion were applied
to psychological testing in general, essentially no tests would be
considered useful. In any case, with a correlation in the order of
0.4, the tests will do an imperfect job of selection. People who
should be rejected will be passed and vice versa.

We know of no organization in the country that has adequately
validated a programmer's aptitude test. Validation means that a
group of prospective employees would be given the test — but the
test results would be completely ignored. Instead the employees
would be hired on some other basis entirely, given the training, and
put to work. Then, a year or so later, the test scores would be dug
out and compared with supervisors' ratings of job performance as a
measure of the tests' effectiveness. No organization has done this
to our knowledge. Instead they have used the test scores in the selection procedure on the assumption that "the tests are probably useful."

In addition to the shortcomings in the selection procedure, the
training of novices poses some problems, A one- or two-week pro-

gramming course, followed by six months of on-the-job training, may be adequate for the conversion of routine record-keeping operations to the computer. With the dramatic increase in complexity that is arriving with the third generation of computers, a short programming course will not be sufficient. This will be particularly true when new techniques that will reduce the role of the applications programmer are used; the newly hired person will have to begin on system-type work. System training cannot be presented in as "canned" a fashion as programming.

We have described the results of training your own staff, in its starkest form. The picture will not get this bad overnight. Companies will continue to use the staffing procedures that have worked well for them in recent years. The point is that within three years or so we believe that such companies will begin to find themselves in trouble, as the technology races ahead of their staff. Now is the time for data processing management to begin investigating other methods of meeting staff requirements. One of these methods is hiring experienced people from the outside.

Hiring Trained People

If it proves difficult for the existing staff to be trained to meet the new technological requirements, it might be possible to hire a few skilled people to provide technological leadership. How good is this solution?

This is a solution that has been used with some success for some years in the engineering and scientific computing disciplines. Friends of ours have told us that they have not hired any novices for several years; they have hired only experienced programmers. This policy has been partly facilitated by the ups and downs of government contracting in recent years. At almost any time some contractor was reducing staff, and his programmers were looking for other jobs. Starting in late 1965 and early 1966, the market tightened up as fewer cutbacks occurred. The obvious result — companies wanting to hire experienced programmers had to offer higher salaries.

In business data processing the problem will be somewhat different. For one thing, writing machine-language programs for a certain computer will not be the experience desired. Instead companies will be looking for experience in writing programs for on-line systems, in installing data communications systems, or in designing large data files. Such experience will be in very short supply.

Even when a person has obtained valuable experience in one of these new technical areas, we believe that the odds are he will not move to another "using" organization. Instead chances are he will consider joining one of the software companies — or even forming a new company of his own! We will discuss the lure of the software companies shortly.

Another important factor in recruiting outside experience is the normal "flow" of talent in the United States. The general flow is from the southern states (except Florida) to the North, and from the East to the West. This flow can involve specific geographical areas. Computer people often do not want to move just to Los Angeles; rather they want specific areas within Los Angeles, such as Santa Monica. A company in the South trying to hire an experienced man from the North or a company in the mid-West trying to hire an experienced man from California will encounter difficulty.

Suppose that one or more apparently experienced people who are interested in accepting a position with your organization can be located. What selection procedures should be used? One point can be made with emphasis — there is just no use giving them a commonly used programmer's aptitude test as a part of the selection procedure. These people probably have taken the major tests or can get access to test answers. If a well-paying job hinges on a high test score, they may see to it that they know the answers.

Probably the best solution is a procedure used by a friend of ours in hiring experienced programmers for engineering applications. He says that his main step is to "calibrate the references." That is, he not only contacts the references, he finds out just how qualified to judge talent the references themselves are. If a person he respects will give a good recommendation for a prospect, that he considers good evidence. If he cannot obtain that evidence, he tries to find a person he respects who knows at least one of the references submitted by the applicant.

We do not believe that hiring experienced personnel from the outside will be a satisfactory general solution to the staffing problem. The supply of such people will be short in the years just ahead, and their price will be high. If the company lies outside the normal "flow" of talent in the U.S., it may be wasting its time trying to hire

68 MANAGEMENT OF DATA PROCESSING

experienced people. And even when interested people can be found, the technology is so new that it will be quite difficult to "calibrate their references."

Buying Outside Services

The two main sources of outside services in system analysis and programming are the software and consulting firms.

Software Firms. The software firms are emerging as a new industry in the United States; their purpose is the creation of computer programs. Up to now much of their work has been done on a contract basis, but they are beginning to venture into the area of proprietary software which they can sell or lease to customers.

The software firms in general have been formed by skilled computer specialists, and the attempt has been made to staff them with the cream of the computer field. Their objective is to undertake complex computer projects for clients, or to supplement clients' staffs on complex projects. For example, software firms have done much of the programming on some of the advanced military and space projects, on real time systems, and on data communications systems. In addition, they have created program translators — for translating programmer's language into the computer's language — for all of the major computer manufacturers.

The software firms so far have been quite successful in attracting talent because of several features they offer. First, they are run by professionals in the field and staffed by professionals. Thus a skilled computer person knows that he will be working among fellow professionals and for managers who understand his work and his problems. He also sees that he can rise to managerial and even executive levels in such firms, some of which are already at $20 million annual gross sales mark and before 1970 will have passed $50 million. Therefore executive positions are attractive. Some of the software firms offer bonus arrangements for their professionals. These firms have been working on challenging, interesting projects, and all in all they offer quite a bit to the computer professional. As a result they are attracting good people. We would expect to see this flow continue. The major losers of good computer talent would be the using organizations and the computer manufacturers' programming staffs.

The software firms prefer to undertake complete projects for clients. But they will provide "body shopping" services where they provide a specified number of professionals for a specified period of time, to work under the client's direction. They will also provide consulting and advisory services.

One of the advantages of buying such services from a software firm is that the talent is likely to be quite highly professional as well as experienced with the problem at hand. (This is a point that cannot be assumed; it must be checked. We have included references on how to check this point in the bibliography.) So the client may use a software firm to completely implement a complex project or at least to undertake the more difficult aspects of the project. Another advantage of using a software firm is that it will have less impact on the salary structure of the client.

But there is the other side of the coin to consider. Skilled professionals working for the client may be attracted to the software firm, and leave to accept a job with it or another such firm. Also, on the negative side of the picture, the costs of the software firms may seem high. When a reputable software firm submits a job cost estimate, or a fixed price bid, it tries to take into account all of the factors that it knows can arise on such a project. In user organizations, project costs have been notoriously underestimated — and software firms must guard against this if they are to remain in business. Also, user organizations tend to look only at direct programming and system design costs, ignoring overhead, vacations, time off to attend conferences, etc. If a using organization considered all the actual costs of a project, it is likely that these costs would approach those of the software firms.

When all costs *are* taken into account, one would expect that the prices charged by the software firms should be *lower* than users' actual costs, because these firms have more highly skilled people. So far, we have seen no indication of this in the typical case. Instead, the software firms feel that they will do a higher quality job — fewer mistakes, better operating efficiency — at about the same costs as the user's staff would require to do a lower quality job.

To date, most of the experience of the software firms — at least, in business-type projects — has been in the programming function. They have not as yet done much in system analysis and system design. But they are anxious to broaden their services into these areas.

One software firm is actively searching to acquire a medium-sized consulting firm, for instance, to build up their capability in management consulting.

The software firms will play an increasingly important role, during the next few years at least, in the implementation of complex computer projects, in our opinion. This is a means of staffing such projects that data processing management should investigate.

Consultants. Consulting services in business-data processing are provided by the major management-consulting firms, the major CPA firms, by specialized EDP consulting firms and by individual consultants.

Unlike the software firms, the consulting firms have specialized (as far as EDP is concerned) in the areas of system analysis, and system design, functions that preceed programming. Most of them do not provide any programming services, or if they do, they provide only one or two people at a time to work with the client's staff. (There are some notable exceptions; a few of the major firms do provide broad programming services.) The reasoning behind this policy is that programming is too routine, and does not fit in with the high executive image that the consulting firms prefer to foster. At present, then, the consulting firms complement, more than compete with, the software firms.

It is not clear just how long the consulting firms will continue to follow this policy, if they want to stay in EDP consulting and if the software firms broaden their services into the systems area.

Consultants often act in an advisory capacity, helping to guide data processing management in planning and directing data processing projects. And the larger consulting firms at least like to provide a few staff members essentially full time during the system analysis and system design phases of a project, to work with the client's staff. These consulting firms generally prefer to undertake a compete system-analysis and system-design project with participation by the client's staff. The reason is that otherwise their report, incorporating their recommendations, is likely to just gather dust because no one in the client organization really understands it.

Users often call consultants in at critical points in a project, to check progress and future plans. Consultants are also called in to review computer manufacturers' bids and provide an objective recommendation. Neither of these uses of consultants is satisfactory. It is unrealistic to call in a consultant for one or two days and expect him to review months of progress and months of future plans. The consultant must spend enough time with the project to be quite familiar with it before he can do an effective job of advising. We have encountered cases in our personal experiences where even one day a month was not enough to let the consultant keep up-to-date on the project.

For selecting equipment, we have already mentioned our preference for mechanized evaluation. In fact, we feel that the bidding process generally is wasteful, time consuming, and inaccurate. The client will be time and money ahead to buy the services of a mechanized computer evaluation service, rather than to have consultants check manufacturers' bids.

General Observations

Staffing will continue to be a major problem for data processing management. There are serious shortcomings in all of the staffing methods we have discussed, which means that there is no easy, ready answer. Data processing management should not assume that selecting and training novices, and upgrading existing staff will provide adequate staffing in the years just ahead. Some other means to supplement the staff seems to be required.

In fact, data processing management should recognize the strong appeal of the software firms for the computer professionals. It is unlikely that a skilled computer professional can get the same combination of financial reward, challenging work, and opportunity for promotion in a using (or even in a computer manufacturing) organization. So the good people may go, leaving a staff of the less skilled and less talented people to handle the more complex projects that are coming up.

It does not appear realistic to expect to meet critical staff needs by recruiting experienced people from other organizations. This solution may prove practical in isolated cases, but we do not see it working as a general solution. The computer professionals are in an excellent bargaining position and they know it. They not only are looking for good financial rewards, challenging work, and a chance for promotion, they are also looking to improve their living environment. It will be very difficult to recruit good people when these conditions cannot be met on a competitive basis.

The software firms are emerging as a feasible solution to the staffing problem. They have the experienced talent and they are likely to get even a higher percentage of it. Soon their services will cover a broad spectrum, from management consulting through to the complete implementation of complex projects.

It looks to us as though the management-consulting firms will not be much more of a solution to the staffing problem than they already are unless they broaden their services to include project implementation. The whole field of management consulting continues to grow, and the major firms may choose to retain their policies of "no programming or anything like it" and still see their over-all business grow.

ACTION THAT CAN BE TAKEN NOW

The best of the solutions to meeting EDP staffing problems (particularly in system analysis and programming) during the next few years appear to be (a) upgrading the present staff, and (b) making greater use of outside services, particularly the software firms. Here are some suggestions on action that can be taken now in connection with these two solutions.

Upgrading the Present Staff. As we pointed out earlier in this chapter, training courses and training material for upgrading an organization's present staff are in very short supply. So the best answer seems to be: plan and implement your own training program.

If longer-range plans for data processing have been laid out — and we argued for such plans in Chapter 2 — then these plans will help determine just what training is needed. If, for instance, plans exist to install a fast response order-entry system in about two years, then it would be wise to begin *now* upgrading the staff for this project.

One approach that we have seen work is to set aside one hour a morning for one or two mornings a week, in which the system and programming staff gets together. Subject areas should be assigned to staff members for investigation, on as voluntary a basis as possible — because they should do these investigations on their own time. For example, a fast-response order-entry system could be broken down into its constituent systems and programming elements. A staff member investigating one element would think about the problem, read the literature, perhaps attend professional meetings on the subject, and consult people in other companies who have installed systems. He would then write up a brief report on the complexities he has uncovered and offer solutions. One or two such reports can be presented at each morning meeting. It is surprising how quickly a body of knowledge builds up. If the reports are reproduced and handed out, they will soon form an impressive collection of knowledge.

Staff members could attend special courses and conferences that deal with the areas being investigated. They can report on the main points learned at such courses and conferences during the regular morning meetings; their notes, conference proceedings, and printed course material can become a part of the department's library.

Also, consideration should be given to bringing in someone experienced in a pertinent topic — say the programming of fast response systems — on a consulting basis. In addition to regular consulting with data processing management, he could give an impromptu talk to the staff at their regular morning meeting and answer questions they might have. Such a talk would probably have more value after the morning meetings had been conducted for some time because the staff members would then have some knowledge of the subject.

A university or consulting group could be asked to arrange a special series of lectures on topics of interest to your group. For instance, one large corporation has arranged with a major university to put on an intensive *eight*-week course on information systems and management science. Selected members of middle management have been attending the course.

The staff might also be encouraged to sit for the Data Processing Management Association's Certificate in Data Processing, on a voluntary basis. The CDP program was designed to encourage education in the data processing field. For its first three years the CDP operated under the "grandfather" concept — people already active in the field could obtain the certificate if they had sufficient experience in the field and could pass a three-hour examination. But now certain educational requirements have been imposed, including courses oriented toward data processing. And it is possible that either the certificate examination will be made more rigorous or that additional examinations will be offered in specialized areas — or both. It would seem that the DPMA Certificate program will develop into a very useful mechanism for upgrading staff members.

Making Greater Use of Outside Services. As we have pointed out, we believe that computer users will find it increasingly advantageous to call on outside professional help in connection with their more advanced, more complex projects.

One way to begin using such services is in connection with the training program discussed above. A consultant (from either a consulting firm or a software firm) experienced in an advanced topic of interest — say, the design of fast response order entry systems — could be brought in for a day to talk to senior staff people. During this visit he could make suggestions on the over-all training program for that subject, helping to break it down into its constituent elements, suggesting sources of information, and perhaps suggesting when he or other outside speakers might best participate.

It would be well also to begin talking to these organizations in connection with projects currently in the backlog, which cannot be tackled as soon as desired because of staff limitations. It is possible that the estimated cost submitted for such projects will seem too high; this high cost may be because the consultants do not fully understand the job and protect themselves be allowing good safety factors. The more precise a definition of the job they receive, the more precise will be their cost estimates.

In the bibliography, we have listed references to literature discussing how to make the most effective use of these outside services. For an ill-defined project, the best way is to employ the consulting organization initially on a per-diem or time-and-materials basis, for a limited period of time. The objective of this first phase is to lay out the whole project in more detail and to define the second phase quite precisely. If the second phase is well defined, the consultants can give a fixed-price bid for performing it, or at least can provide a range within which they will work. At the end of the second phase, the third phase (if needed) should be well defined, so that again a firm price can be given.

One problem of using a consulting organization (and this includes software firms) on projects is that the consultant's staff does not want to spend much time at the client's place of business — particularly if travel away from home is involved. Good project control is essential in such cases because "absentee" programmers tend to make their own decisions on the processing logic for unusual conditions, since it is inconvenient to check with the client's staff. If program logic has been specified in decision-table form (which we discuss more in the next chapter) and checked with line managers in the client company, then this risk will be greatly reduced.

These, then, are steps that can be taken now in order to get ready for the shortage of skilled personnel that looms ahead.

5 The Changing Technology: Its Implications

In this chapter we will review some of the ways in which the changing technology is affecting management's decisions on data processing. The changes in the technology generally have the effect of making available possibilities and adding alternatives, thus complicating decision making.

Reduced Costs of Computation. We mentioned at the beginning of the book, in connection with the outstanding characteristics of data processing, that the costs of computation and of data storage are being reduced at a remarkable rate. For instance, the cost of computation (the operations performed internally in the computer) is being reduced at an average rate of about 40 per cent per year. That is, as new computers or new models of existing computers are announced, their price-performance characteristics exhibit this reduction.

Not all of this reduced cost is passed along to the user in the form of reduced data processing expenses. Instead, the computer is called upon to do more. Most of the third-generation computers will use *operating systems* — software programs that perform the routine functions of storing and retrieving data, checking for and attempting to correct data errors, controlling the sequence in which jobs are performed, and so on. These operating systems relieve both operators and programmers of a large number of routine functions; they become a necessity when multiprogramming is used — where the computer operates on more than one job concurrently. The price for this assistance is paid both in storage, for storing the operating-system programs, and in the operating time required to execute these programs — and currently this price is relatively high. But even with such offsetting factors, the trend of computation costs is definitely down.

As computation costs become, say, one half, one fifth, or one tenth of what they were in 1960, this means that they become less significant relative to other costs. By the end of this decade, computation costs may well be in the order of 1 per cent of what they were in 1960. With this reduction, computer time really becomes a resource of secondary importance relative to other resources such as system-analyst time and programmer time. If techniques can be used which will help to reduce system analyst time and programmer time, perhaps at the expense of computer time, they should certainly be considered.

Reduced costs of computation result in functions being converted to the computer which previously were considered economically unjustified. Similarly, programming techniques can be used which might be considered less efficient in their use of computer time but much more efficient in their demands on system analyst or programmer time.

A good example of a function that is becoming economically feasible is the retention of detailed historical transaction data in machine language. Ten years ago, every effort was made to minimize the amount of data retained in magnetic tape files, because every extra data character carried in a record represented a measurable extra cost. Now it is becoming feasible to retain literally hundreds of thousands or millions of detailed transactions in machine language for some period of time. Such data will be most useful in a management reporting system. It helps to answer such questions as: When did this unsatisfactory condition really start? Where did it start? Did such-and-such a condition exist last year? What has been the trend in such-and-such over the past two years? Reduced costs of computation are making it feasible to both retain and process such historical data.

Emerging Computing Utilities. The concept of the computing utility is that a large central computer complex, coupled with a powerful software repertoire, can serve many users scattered over a wide geographical area. Each user would have one or more input-output terminals, connected to the central computer by a data communications line. These terminals either may be continuously connected to the computer, through the use of leased communications lines, or the connection may be established only when needed by using the telephone dial network. Even if the terminals are connected via leased lines, they make no demands on the computer until input data is entered or until the computer has some output data for them. In short, the user uses the system only when he needs it, and pays only for the amount he actually uses it.

↦ A pioneering computing utility is Keydata Corporation in Cambridge, Massachusetts, which was dedicated in late 1965. Keydata was set up to provide data processing services to smaller businesses in the Boston area — for example, inventory control and customer billing for wholesale liquor firms. As both Keydata and its potential customers began to analyze the market more deeply, it became apparent that the Keydata system could serve a broader range of enterprises; for example, a large firm, or several small ones, in North Carolina could economically justify use of the Keydata services in Boston if some twenty terminal devices in the North Carolina area could share communications line charges. Large companies began also to consider the service as a means of quickly getting an on-line system into operation. Even though the bulk of their data processing might be done on their own system, they found that they could consider Keydata for specialized fast response functions.

General Electric has utility services on the air. Western Union is well along in the development of a nationwide computing utility. International Telephone and Telegraph is pioneering in this field. Many people in the field expect IBM, Univac, RCA, and the other computer manufacturers to enter this market shortly. Some software firms will probably enter it.

The basic decision facing management in this area soon will be: do we want to retain our own computer, or do we want to get rid of it and use a computing utility? The advantages of the computing utility are numerous. For one thing, the computing utility can provide a much more powerful computer and software repertoire to users than most users can economically provide for themselves. Although a small user may seldom use the full power of the system, still the power is there when he needs it. Also, the computing utilities will provide already prepared application packages, drastically cutting implementation time and costs. If the user wants special features in his programs, he is charged for the implementation costs to install them. The computing utility promises to have a talented staff and may do some of the user's programming, thus relieving the staffing problem for the user.

From the financial point of view, the utility permits a user to start using a computer with very low initial costs. Equipment selection and installation and much software development is done by the utility. But operating costs are higher. This is partly because the time-shared mode of operation involves reduced efficiency and partly because the utility must cover its overhead (and, if a separate enterprise, its profit). For the small user with limited capital or when the computer system must be demonstrated before the capital can be expended, utilities make good financial sense.

We have more to say on the concept of the computing utility in the next chapter and so will limit our discussion of it at this point. It is desirable to at least metion some of the problems that these new utilities will face, though, problems of which data processing management should be aware. One key point is data security. Technically this problem does exist, although considerable progress has been made toward solving it. Techniques are available for safeguarding against intrusion of privacy and against data destruction. But many potential users single out this reason, data security, to rationalize why they do not want to use the computing utility. They may have not really investigated to see how secure their data would be when using a utility; they just do not want to lose their own computer, and hold this up as the reason.

Conceivably, a computing utility could become so overloaded during peak load periods that a user's service becomes unsatisfactory. A utility will have to design for *some* peak load — and circumstances can arise which will cause demand to exceed that peak. True, some computation problems can be "shipped" to another utility — via data communications — but it is unlikely that file-oriented jobs (plus the files) can be moved quickly. The same peak-load problem can hold true of a utility's programming staff — unless the utilities will encourage users to do much of their own programming.

The solutions to such problems already in use are adequate for users' present requirements, as indicated in talks with users. As new requirements arise, we expect that they will be solved because the utilities are being staffed by highly qualified people. The *types* of problems they face are really no different from the types of problems faced by computer users all along.

We foresee the rapid growth of the computing utilities in the next decade. At this point in time, we can only "guesstimate," but it looks to us as though computing utilities may perform in the order of one-half of the data processing workload in the United States by 1975. Until then, the individual installations will probably be carrying the bulk of the load.

If anything like this rate of growth materializes, data processing managements will have to start considering computing utilities in their long-range planning within the next three or four years.

Possible Separation of Hardware and Software Prices. The data processing field has been conditioned to expect the computer manufacturer to supply valuable software free of extra charge. In the mid-1950's, such software was very rudimentary — utility routines for transferring data from one tape to another, and such. Shortly thereafter, the manufacturers began to supply general-purpose sort programs, and software (assemblers) for translating the programmer's language to machine language. Shortly after that, the manufacturers began providing higher level translators (compilers) for translating higher-level languages such as COBOL to machine language. Next came the early application packages — "canned" programs for doing payrolls, billing, and so on. Continued improvements have been made in the application packages, to allow them to have wider applicability. And as mentioned above, the third-generation computers will make extensive use of operating systems, again supplied by the computer manufacturers. Finally, new programming" languages are being developed — such as PL/1, Generalized Information System, and IMRADS — and the manufacturers are supplying both the new languages and the translators for them — all free of extra charge. This is probably the biggest "giveaway" in history. How can it be justified?

Obviously, the cost to the manufacturers of developing software keeps going up and up, because more software is being developed and it is more complex. Part of this increased cost is spread over the larger number of computers in the field. But we suspect that the lion's share of the increased cost is being paid for out of savings from reduced hardware-production costs. New engineering and production techniques, such as integrated circuits, are cutting engineering costs and production costs drastically. What is saved on the hardware is being spent on the software, to a considerable degree, in our estimation.

What this amounts to is that the computer manufacturers now have a large captive software market, representing a significant portion of their gross incomes. The user is paying for the manufacturer's software whether he wants it or not. It is possible — and this would be a hard point to prove — that software costs now represent over 50 per cent of the rental or purchase price charged to the customer. Software supplied by the computer manufacturer at no extra charge probably could be defended during the formative years of the field. The average user had more questions than answers about the use of this new equipment; moreover, most application programmers did not (and do not) have the talent to write general-purpose software. Also, the software that was supplied was not a large cost burden for the manufacturer.

Now the picture is changing. Users are more sophisticated; it is not unusual for large companies to have a number of programmers capable of writing software. The independent software companies are emerging, and they can develop software to meet a user's specific requirements. Proprietary software is being developed and offered for sale by these independent software companies, as well as by users themselves. It would appear that it is becoming less and less in the interests of the user to maintain the status quo — that is, the combined hardware and software prices.

At the same time, it is becoming more and more *in* the interests of the computer manufacturers to maintain this status quo. The hidden but effective "sale" of software to this captive software market continues to represent an increasing portion of their gross incomes. If hardware and software prices were to be separated, and if the manufacturers lost a good percentage of their software business, their gross incomes could be severely hurt.

Will the prices of hardware and software be separated within the next five years or so? There are many "ifs" on both sides of the question. But we feel that this separation is more in the interests of the user with each passing day and that the field will soon have to acknowledge this reality.

Regardless of whether or not these prices are separated, data processing management will have to become accustomed to buying software. Good proprietary software is already on the market; more is sure to come. Smart users are seeing that the sale of software offers another form of income. Data processing management simply cannot rest on the policy that "we expect to get all our software free from the manufacturer." The field is progressing too rapidly for that policy to be valid much longer.

SELECTING EQUIPMENT, SOFTWARE, AND METHODS

Equipment and Related Software

Equipment selection for data processing used to be a relatively easy decision — and software selection was even easier. A professional job of equipment selection involved laying out a set of specifications that defined the job to be done and then timing out a variety of computer configurations against this workload. Often users would define a workload that they wanted performed in one shift; extra shifts would then be used to undertake additional work and to absorb any errors of estimate made on the original workload. Once the equipment had been selected, such a paucity of business-oriented software existed for it that most of the time the software decisions were trivial.

Occasionally, however, the software decisions were not trivial. Take, for example, the decision on whether to use COBOL or an assembly language as the programming language. Both have been offered with most second generation computers. At least one computer manufacturer apparently viewed COBOL as a threat; if users started programming in COBOL, they could more easily switch programs to another make of machine, in the eyes of this manufacturer. So this manufacturer's representatives talked down COBOL as being inefficient and less practical. (Sure enough, some of this manufacturer's translators — for translating COBOL to machine language — *were* pretty bad.) Because data processing management often delegated the decision on programming languages to the programmers, the manufacturer's arguments proved convincing. The result has been that the conversion of programs to the third-generation computers has been made considerably more costly and drawn out for the users who followed this advice.

Now the decisions on the equipment and its related software (such as the operating system) are becoming much more complex, with a larger penalty attached to a wrong decision. First of all, there is a much larger variety of equipment. Not only do the major computer manufacturers offer very competive equipment, but even within a single manufacturer the number of alternatives is greater. The user may choose from a variety of models and internal memory sizes. He may choose magnetic tape or mass storage — or a wide variety of combinations of them — for data storage. He may choose to install a data communications system — and must decide whether the communications computer will be a separate computer or whether its functions will be performed by a regular data processing computer. He must decide what communications lines he will use — lower cost and slower teletypewriter lines, faster and more expensive telephone lines, or fastest and most expensive broadband leased lines. And not too far in the future, data communications via satellite to any major point on the earth should be a reality.

In addition, there is a growing variety of software systems. The third generation is made up of families of computers that are reasonably compatible from the smallest to the largest — "compatible" meaning that in theory the same programs can run on all members of the family. But in fact the larger members of a family *are* different — usually with more internal memory, often with specific additional hardware features. The result is that there develops a family of software systems for a family of computers — more limited software for the smaller models, more sophisticated software for the larger models. A user may well find that the software characteristics he wants are available only with the larger models of computers than he really needs. So software may have a big bearing on the selection of equipment.

But the problem does not end there. Coupled with this variety of equipments and software systems is a growing variety of system designs. The days are gone when batch processing of magnetic tape files was the only thing that a system designer really had to consider. True, batch processing will continue to be done — and probably to a very sizable extent — and magnetic tapes will continue to be a major form of data storage. But some of the applications will be performed on a fast response basis. Management may soon want to see reports presented via CRT-type consoles, and later via large-screen displays; this implies fast response operation. The system designer is then faced with the question: how are the batch operations and fast response operations best handled? Should we have one fast computer that works on the batch jobs on a low priority basis, and is interrupted when necessary by the fast response jobs? Or should we have a smaller computer, do the fast response jobs during the regular working hours, and do the batch jobs at night? Or should we have two separate computers, perhaps identical, one for the fast response applications and one for the batch jobs? These are only a few of the many alternatives available in system design.

The old ways of manually laying out one or two system designs and then manually timing out several computer configurations against these designs — these old ways just aren't practical with the number of alternatives now available. To be honest about it, the field does not yet have a really effective way of coping with this problem. The number of possible alternatives is too large and the complexity of considering each alternative is too great to say that simply mechanizing this process will solve it. What we can say is that, although mechanized procedures fall short of the ideal, they are substantially better than the old manual methods.

A few of the computer manufacturers have developed programs for mechanized evaluation — that is, for timing out a computer configuration against a series of workloads. As far as a user is concerned, this mechanized evaluation is limited to that manufacturer's products, and even then the evaluation can be superficial, ignoring some of the subtle points that really ought to be considered.

Let us describe an actual instance, to illustrate the value of mechanized evaluations. In this instance, a client obtained bids from several computer manufacturers, where the bids were to be based on a well-defined workload. In this workload, some of the data records were specified to be over eleven hundred characters in length, although the average length was only about four hundred characters. One of the manufacturers, in preparing his bid, used only the average record lengths, since the equipment could obviously handle the maximum lengths. This was a reasonable assumption under the old manual way of timing runs. As it was, the manufacturer's systems engineer who prepared the bid spent many

night and week-end hours on it — and this was a major manufacturer and the time was 1963.

But the bids were checked by the use of SCERT, a mechanized
evaluation system. And SCERT detected something that the systems engineer had overlooked.

The software package for this particular computer could not
handle any records the way that the systems engineers had assumed
it could, if *some* of the records were more than 1000 characters
in length. Without correcting this, the time for this part of the
workload would be about three times greater than the manufacturer's estimate. To correct this, either the file arrangement had to
be changed to reduce maximum record lengths or special software
had to be obtained. A small point, but it had a big effect on times
and costs.

Manual timing methods are slow, inaccurate, expensive, and do
not allow us to consider a sufficient number of different system
designs and equipment configurations. Mechanized evaluation is a
major improvement. In fact, we are of the opinion that users would
do well to avoid asking manufacturers to submit bids or proposals
on the *equipment*. Instead, have the equipment evaluations performed by an objective mechanized evaluation service. True, such
a service is at the expense of the user — but he will be time and
money ahead because of the notoriously poor results of the bidding
process. (We have personally reviewed scores of bids over the
years, and we make this statement without hesitation.)

If the computer manufacturer is not called in to propose equipment, how *do* you deal with him? Have the manufacturer submit
a bid on what he has to offer in auxiliary services rather than on
the equipment itself. Have him describe the true compatibility of
his family of machines — that is, just how well can a user expand
his computer, or move to a faster and larger model, without having
to change his programs? Can the manufacturer provide an emergency backup service, in case the user's computer is down for an
extended period — and if so, where will it be provided? Where will
the user's programmers have to go to test programs before the new
computer arrives? How many site representatives will the manufacturer provide, for how long, for what percentage of their working
hours, and what will be their qualifications? What training courses
will the manufacturer provide, when, and how often will they be

repeated at the convenience of the user? What software does the manufacturer have available or in the late stages of development *that is specifically pertinent to the user?* (Check into this point carefully. The salesman will claim all sorts of great things, but often they turn out to be inapplicable for a given user.) What financing alternatives are provided — renting, long term leasing, outright purchase, conditional sales contract, trade-in of a purchased computer? And, of course, the manufacturer must provide the hardware and software specifications, for the mechanized evaluation.

The manufacturer can and should provide this information. What the manufacturer has *not* been doing really well is to tell you what equipment you should use, how much time it will take to do your workload, and what it will cost you.

Note that using a computing utility means the user avoids these selection problems.

Software Selection

Until quite recently the user has had few alternatives available when it came to software, so that the problem of selection has been a small one. As mentioned just above, most business users have had an opportunity to choose between COBOL and an assembly-type programming language. (A few businesses have used FORTRAN for data processing.) Some of the recent COBOL translators are quite good; this fact, coupled with the need to convert programs to the third-generation computers, has accelerated the acceptance and use of COBOL.

Once a user has decided to use COBOL, there usually is no choice on which COBOL translator to use. We are familiar with only one model of computer that in 1966 had the choice of two COBOL translators, both of which were supplied by the computer manufacturer. One of these translators was one of the first ones written and is quite inefficient. The second is one of the best translators now available, but requires a somewhat larger complement of equipment — that is, more internal memory in the computer, and more magnetic tape units. Users of this computer, if they have the equipment to handle the second translator, obviously use it in preference to the first.

In the scientific and engineering computing areas users have had more alternatives in higher level language translators. One family of computers has had two FORTRAN translators available, one supplied free of extra charge by the computer manufacturer, and the other leased by an independent software company. The same situation has prevailed in the case of translators for SIMSCRIPT, a programming language for writing simulation programs. You might ask how an independent software company can sell or lease such a product when the computer manufacturer supplies the same product at no extra charge. The answer is that the products are not the same. To sell, the translators supplied by these independent software companies must be faster and more efficient than the ones supplied by the computer manufacturers. Enough computer time must be saved, both in translating and operating, to pay for the cost of the purchased translators.

This same condition should develop in the business data processing field, not only for program translators but also for other types of software. In some cases, users and software companies have developed sort and merge programs that are much more efficient than those supplied by the computer manufacturer — and have offered these programs for sale or lease. Computer manufacturers and others are developing application packages ("canned" programs for performing an application), and users will have the choice of using such application packages or custom-making their own programs. As mentioned earlier, the independent software companies can be expected to bring out more proprietary software aimed at the business field. All of these developments will result in an increase in the number of alternatives available to the user. And more alternatives mean more complex decisions.

The user's selection problem will often be complicated because the software is still being developed. He will have to make a decision based only on the published software characteristics, not the finished software packages themselves. But the almost universal experience with software has been that it is "late, limited, and leaky." Because the field is still in the "Middle Ages" with respect to software production — that is, it is still created by hand, by artisans, in much the same way that shoes were made by hand in the Middle Ages — it is subject to human frailties during its production. Generally, software is not ready for delivery on the date when it was first promised. And when it is finally delivered, the first version does not include some of the desirable features on which the user was counting; such features are delayed until a later version. And even though the first version is a limited one, users often detect a number of errors in it during the early stages of use.

As alternative software packages become available, the field will be faced with the need for developing methods for specifying software. Currently we know of no such methods comparable to those available for specifying hardware. Software packages for a specific application probably will not be identical in the functions they perform. The user should have a ready means of comparing the functions performed by the alternative packages, and it is hoped that some standards for software descriptions will be developed.

Another alternative open to the user will be the modification of existing software to better serve his needs. This is a controversial subject. With some software packages, the supplier (today, usually the computer manufacturer) is continually releasing improved versions of each package. It is not unusual, for instance, for program translators to have twenty or thirty versions — and the user is expected to be using the most recent version. If the user modifies Version 15, for instance, to better meet his needs, and writes his programs to take advantage of these modifications, then he is faced with making the same modifications to Version 16, 17, and so on, as they are released. It would be much more desirable, of course, if the supplier could make all changes so that the user did not have to, and to a certain extent this practice is followed. But with a large number of users, each with his own ideas of improvements, this practice cannot be followed completely.

If the prices of hardware and software are separated, so that users must purchase software — and must purchase the improved versions of each package — then more stability may enter the picture. Users will be more inclined to continue using the version they have purchased, rather than buying each new version as it is released. They will look at the software more like hardware. The longer they continue to use a piece of software, the more reasonable it is that they will modify it to meet their specific requirements. And software manufacturers will be more careful of changing a software package that is in wide use.

How will the selection be performed, when choosing between alternative software packages? The three most likely methods are:

compare their characteristics, simulate their performance, and actually test their performance. As we mentioned, the field does not yet have a reference in which a standard set of characteristics is published for each piece of software. Such a reference is available for hardware, in the form of the *Auerbach Standard EDP Reports* (which also covers software, but only in a very limited way). Since the number of different software packages is already large, and becoming larger rapidly, perhaps such a reference for software will have to be mechanized. That is, instead of the information being printed and supplied in notebook form, the information will be retained in a computer. The users will make inquiries to this reference computer, possibly by teletypewriter, and receive an immediate response.

Simulation can be used to check the combined performance of hardware and software — for example, the combination of a computer and its operating system, or the computer, its operating system, and the programming language used. The use of simulation will provide the user with more information about the software package than will a table of characteristics. It will tell him more about the dynamics of the combined hardware-software system. The problem, of course, will be in trying to extend this technique to cover the many types of software that will be available for the many types of computers. For some time to come, at least, simulation probably will be applied mostly to the most basic software such as operating systems and program translators, and will not be used much on the multiplicity of application packages.

It appears to us that the main selection mechanism that will be used in the years just ahead will be by actual test of the software in the computer. Some alternative software packages may be eliminated by a study of their published characteristics. But in the final analysis, data processing management will prefer to make a decision between two or more closely competing packages on the basis of actual performance in the machine, where this is practical. This means that a new cost account code will have to be set up, to which personnel and computer time are charged — the evaluation of software.

For the selection of software, then, we hope to see some form of standard reference created, from which the characteristics of alternative software packages can be quickly and easily compared

— just as exists today for computer hardware. Such a standard reference will aid in the initial selection of the software. Once the number of alternatives has been narrowed down, the next step would seem to be an actual test of the hardware-software combination, or a simulation of their performance where an actual test is not feasible.

There is not even a single central reference or "purchasing guide" which can be used to locate the existence of a software package to do a particular job on the equipment available. An extensive search must be made of the manufacturer's packages, other users, universities, and software firms to locate the packages that might be useful — if there are any.

Selecting Implementation Methods

Several new techniques well along in development promise to have an important impact on the speed with which jobs can be converted to the computer. We have mentioned these from time to time in previous chapters, and would now like to discuss them in more detail. These techniques are:

- Generalized file processing software
- Decision tables
- Application packages
- Time-shared systems

Generalized File-Processing Software. Business data ordinarily is organized into data files, whether the data is stored on paper, in punched cards, or on some magnetized media. Businesses have customer files, inventory files, open purchase-order files, accounts receivable, and so on.

Regardless of the contents of the file or the type of medium on which the data is stored, there are a number of basic operations that are performed on all files. Some of these concepts have come into clearer focus as we have converted data files to a magnetic medium, for use with electronic data processing. So, while we will talk about these functions in the environment of EDP, they could be discussed in terms of paper files or punched card files.

One obvious function that must be performed is file creation. Data must be converted to machine language, the validity of each data field must be established, such as has an alphabetic character by mistake been written into an amount field or does an amount field exceed some prescribed upper limit? The data fields must be put into the prescribed sequence in the data records. The records themselves must be entered into the file according to a prescribed sequence or record linking scheme. This function of file creation is needed when a new data file is first being set up, and it is also needed whenever new records must be entered into an existing file.

Another common function is called *file maintenance*. This function includes the mechanics of inserting new records into a file (making space for them and providing a means of retrieving them), deleting obsolete records from a file, inserting new fields in data records or deleting obsolete fields, or replacing the current value of a data field with an incoming value. This function involves no arithmetic processing of the records, but rather just the logical operations of insertion, deletion, and replacement.

Another common function is sorting. Sometimes incoming records must be sorted, so as to be in the same sequence as the file — such as sorting new customer orders by customer name or number. Sometimes records that have been retrieved from a file have to be sorted for the preparation of a report. Even though computer salesmen claim that their company's new mass storage device eliminates the need for sorting, don't believe it. The field has not yet found a way to eliminate all need for sorting.

Another common function is data retrieval, which breaks down into selection and extraction. When we desire to obtain some information from a file, we, in effect, ask for a search of the file, based on some criteria we supply. One common and simple type of search criterion is: find the data record for Customer A, or for Part Number X. A more complex search criterion is: how many employees are there in this company who are male, between the ages of 27 and 35, have a masters degree in engineering or science, and who can speak French? In the first example, the computer either searches through the file sequentially until it comes to the desired record, or it refers to an index which tells where the desired record is stored. In the more complex example, the computer must examine every record in the file, or must examine different indexes or linkage chains that list everyone with a master's degree, everyone who speaks French, etc.

Once the records that meet the criteria have been located, it is necessary to extract data from those records. For example, find the data record for Customer A and extract from it the dollar value of all outstanding orders. Or, having located the employee records that meet the abovementioned criteria, extract each employee's name, department number, highest college degree, field, and age.

Another common function is report preparation. Having selected and extracted desired data from the file (or perhaps from more than one file), we may want to sort it, summarize it, and then display it in an easily understood format, with appropriate symbols, arrangement and headings. Today, the most common means of display is via the high-speed printer. With the arrival of fast response systems, teletypewriters and CRT-type displays will be used. Whatever the means of display, we want the information presented to us in a form that we can easily comprehend.

The discussion above summarizes the common file-processing functions that are involved in the use of all data files. Every record-keeping application of EDP has used them. And practically every record-keeping application of EDP has handled these functions on a custom-made basis. Programmers have "reinvented these wheels" thousands upon thousands of times. And the programming of these functions has represented a very sizable portion of total programming time.

A number of people in the field almost simultaneously have come to the conclusion that it would be preferable to write generalized routines for performing these common functions. These generalized routines would include all the subroutines that experience has shown to be most widely useful; in a given case, the "programmer" would specify which of those subroutines applied. True, these generalized routines might not be quite as efficient in their use of computer storage and computer time as the best custom-made routines, but then how many "best" programmers does an installation have? And anyway, why be so concerned with computer costs, since they are becoming a secondary factor?

Development in these generalized file processing techniques is well along. Informatics, Inc., a prominent independent software firm, has marketed several systems for the IBM 1401-1410 series of machines. Scientific Data Systems, Inc. has developed MANAGE, quite similar in concept to the Informatics packages. IBM has been developing Generalized Information System (GIS), which can handle more functions than the ones listed above. GE has developed Integrated Data Store (IDS), a very powerful system. Univac has Information Management Retrieval and Dissemination System (IMRADS), under development, which again does more than the functions listed above. Control Data Corporation is developing INFOL; National Cash Register has BEST. System Development Corporation in Santa Monica has a prototype system TSS-LUCID in operation, and is well along in developing another, TDMS. We could go on, but these brief references should indicate that much work is being done.

Up to the time of writing, most of the generalized functions had been developed for magnetic-tape files, since the handling of these files is quite well understood. Some work has been done in developing generalized file-processing routines for batch-processed files stored in mass storage devices. Many of these routines are similar to those used with magnetic tape, but some important changes are imposed by the characteristics of mass storage. A small amount of development work has been done on the fast-response handling of files in mass storage, especially in the functions of selection, extraction, and display of data. We should repeat that these generalized file-processing software systems are in the late stages of development, as this is written, and are not yet in wide use.

Early experience has indicated that where these generalized techniques apply (such as, for batch-processed files), "programming time" can be cut to a small fraction of what it is normally. For files in which little arithmetic manipulation must be done, such as personnel, the time required to create the programs may be 1 per cent to 10 per cent of the time required to write tailor-made programs in an assembly-level language. Most files require processing and arithmetic manipulation — processing a payroll file, updating an inventory file, or accounts receivable file. In such cases the generalized routines apply to perhaps 40 to 60 per cent of the total programs. Programming time is substantially reduced but not eliminated.

Decision Tables. Decision tables provide a means of expressing defined decision logic in a manner so simple that it is grasped quickly by almost anyone. What we are talking about is a table that expresses the following: If this set of conditions is true, then this set of actions will be taken.

Table 5.1 shows an example of a simple yet typical decision table, applying to the issuance of an insurance policy. Rule 1 states: *if* the number of miles driven per year is under 5000, *and if* the age of the youngest male driver is over 25, *and if* the accident history has been good, *then* the policy limit is 100/300, *and* the rate per $1000 is $1.12 *and* the type of policy is A. Rule No. 2 is similar, but the accident history is medium so that the rate per $1000 goes up to $1.25. And so on for the other rules.

Table 5.1   A Decision Table

	If	And if	And if	Then	And	And
Rule no.	Number of miles driven per year	Age of youngest male driver	Accident history	Policy limit	Rate per $1000	Type of policy
1	Under 5,000	Over 25	Good	100/300	1.12	A
2	Under 5,000	Over 25	Medium	100/300	1.25	A
•	...	...	...	...	...	...
•	...	...	...	...	...	...
•	...	...	...	...	...	...
X	Over 15,000	25 or under	Poor	10/20	2.50	F

Decision tables are so simple in concept that it is surprising that they have not been used more widely and for a longer period. But they were "discovered" for the computer field in the late 1950's, and only now are becoming fairly widely used. One reason for this slow acceptance is that they require a different mental orientation to a problem than does the flow charting approach. System analysts and programmers have been so wedded to the mental orientation of flow charts that they have resisted decision tables.

Decision tables provide a powerful means of studying current operations, of specifying the decision logic that the new system will follow, and of specifying the decision logic of the computer programs. Translating programs are now available which directly convert a decision table into a computer program, bypassing many of the functions performed by the applications programmer. That is, the decision table specifying the logic of a computer program can be developed by a system analyst and easily checked by line management. Once they are satisfied with the logic, the table is punched into punched cards or whatever means is used for entering data into the computer, with perhaps one punched card for each line of the table. The cards are fed into the computer, along with the table translating program. The computer then prepares the new computer program.

Note that the decision tables are aimed directly at the area that the generalized file processing techniques do not cover — the processing logic that is peculiar to the particular application. As such, they make a natural partner for generalized file processing systems. And they can reduce the "programming" time for specifying the decision logic in the same way that the generalized routines cut the "programming" time for file processing functions. We put quotes around "programming" because these two techniques — where they apply — virtually eliminate the function of the applications programmer.

We must note here that of the actual generalized systems listed above, only the Univac IMRADS system so far has attempted to combine these two techniques. But it is so natural and logical a combination that we expect other implementers to follow Univac's lead.

Applications Packages. We have mentioned applications packages several times previously in this book, and have often parenthetically defined them as "canned" programs for an application. But this term "canned" can give the wrong impression of what these packages are becoming.

In the late 1950's and early 1960's, computer manufacturers on numerous occasions were called upon to help a customer program a big application. In some of these cases, the manufacturer volunteered the help, so as to gain experience in the application area — for example, the maintenance of a life insurance policy file. In other cases, the manufacturer had to agree to do a specified part of the programming in order to get the customer's order. The rationale adopted by the computer manufacturer in most of these cases was: We will have rights to these programs and can use them to sell additional computers to other firms in this same business.

But things did not work out quite that way. Usually, when another customer in the same line of business as the first examined the programs, he found that the decision logic did not quite fit his business, as he wanted it conducted. And, upon examination, it was often found that changing the programs to make them suitable might well be more expensive than creating new programs. So these early application packages did not receive wide acceptance.

The next logical step for the computer manufacturers was to create application packages based on studies of a number of firms in the same line of business. The processing logic was set up to handle any case that had been encountered in these firms, either in one large program or in a group of program "modules." Now a customer had a better chance of finding that the application package applied to his business. But if it did not, it might still be a hard job to revise the package or the modules — and possibly less expensive to write custom-made programs. But the picture is changing; some users are now finding that they can use applications packages with relatively few changes required.

But the next logical step for application packages, it seems to us, is to make use of generalized file-processing techniques and decision tables. The applications logic can be expressed in decision-table form. A prospective customer can review these tables relatively easily, and make changes where necessary. The tables can be converted to program form, as discussed above, and this program logic in turn combined with the selected file-processing routines.When the customer had changes to make in a program, he would go through the same steps. We do not want to imply that this approach would be a panacea for all problems, but it should make application packages more flexible and useful.

The use of such applications packages will not only further reduce the role of the applications programmer; it will begin to cut into the role of the system analyst and system designer. Where these people will continue to be needed is in areas where standard solutions have not yet been developed, at the forefront of the field.

Time-Shared Systems. What time-shared systems have to offer, in connection with what we are discussing in this section, is additional power for creating new programs. We foresee time-shared systems — used in conjunction with generalized file-processing software, decision tables, perhaps application packages, and appropriate user "commands" — speeding up even more the process of converting an application to the computer.

Perhaps we can describe this use of time-shared systems best by reviewing what one prototype system already is doing. This is the TSS-LUCID system, developed by the System Development Corporation of Santa Monica, California; TSS-LUCID will soon be supplanted by the Time-Shared Data Management System (TDMS), which will be installed when SDC replaces their old computer with a new third-generation computer. TDMS will extend and improve the concepts that have been proved out with TSS-LUCID.

The user of TSS-LUCID sits at a teletypewriterlike console; by striking specified keys on the keyboard, he notifies the time-shared system that he wants service and that he wants to use the TSS-LUCID system. The time-shared system calls the TSS-LUCID programs into the machine and notifies the user to go ahead. In the SDC case, the user may be the only one using TSS-LUCID or these programs may be in use by others simultaneously. To the time-sharing system, this is just one more job, to be worked on in its proper turn, as computing time is available. Jobs which have no connection with TSS-LUCID may be in process concurrently.

Let us assume that the user wants to extract data from an existing file so as to form a new subfile, which he will then repeatedly interrogate. For the sake of illustration, we will assume that he is extracting all expense-type transactions for a group of departments, for the past six months. Perhaps something has called his attention to the expenses of these departments, and he wants to analyze the expenses to see what is wrong. These transactions are extracted from the file of all historical transactions. We should note here that while TSS-LUCID has been used for performing functions identical in concept to what we are discussing, this example is not based on SDC's use of the system.

To form the subfile, the user informs the system that he wants to create a new file. He uses English-like commands to do this. The system responds by asking him to define the first data field — that is, tell some of its characteristics (alphabetic or numeric, and such). After he has defined the first field in sufficient detail, and the computer has performed some checks on the definition, he is asked to define the second field. The terms "first field" and "second field" are relative — just the sequence in which he happens to define them. But these definitions must agree with the transaction data fields. It usually will take only a short time for the user to define this new file. He then identifies the transaction file from which the desired transactions are to be extracted, as well as the criteria by which the desired transactions will be selected.

The time required for the searching of the transaction file, and the selection and extraction of the desired data depends upon where the transaction data has been stored, and the volume of the transactions. If a magnetic tape has to be removed from the tape vault and mounted on a tape unit, it may be a number of minutes before the search begins. The search time itself depends on how many other people are using the system — in other words, what percentage of the time the computer can work on this job. If a long delay (say, thirty minutes) is involved, the time-sharing system can notify the user so that he does not have to remain at the console.

Once the desired transactions have been selected and extracted, TSS-LUCID forms them into the new file, based on the definition supplied by the user. When the file has been organized — that is, stored according to the procedures used by TSS-LUCID, with indexes developed for all of the data fields — the user can begin asking his questions. He types the questions in on the keyboard. If he wants to know how many transactions in total there are in the new file, he simply types in the word COUNT (a typical command). He may ask for a count of the number of transactions for each department, in almost as simple a manner. He can ask for month-by-month totals of expenses, by department. If one department's expenses looks out of line (the user probably has budget figures at his disposal or can get them from the system), he can ask for a breakdown of that department's expenses by type of expense. Next he may ask for a breakdown of that department's expenses by the different projects on which the department worked. If necessary, he can call for a display of the individual transactions making up a particular expense category. In short, the user can track expense deviations right back to the level of the detailed transactions, if he desires.

The user defines how he wants the information displayed, again by typing rather simple entries into the keyboard. And with the newer TDMS system, these definitions of report formats can be retained, and used in the future in connection with this file.

If the user wants, he could also tell the system to continue adding the new expense transactions for these departments to this subfile, as they occur. He can have new analyses prepared, using the previously-defined report formats — or new formats, if he prefers — whenever he desires. We are not describing a system that may come into being at some unpredictable time in the future; we are describing how a pilot system already in existence is working.

The same approach that we have just described can be used for setting up a completely new application. The major difference might be that the data for a new application would not yet be available to the computer. In this case, the data would have to be gathered, key-punched, and the punched cards fed to the computer. Also, some applications would require that master records be updated by incoming transactions; the system would have to have the procedures necessary to perform the updating. One logical way of entering those procedures, in our opinion, is via the decision-table format. Such systems in the future should provide for entering procedures via decision tables.

Thus TSS-LUCID incorporates the generalized file-processing operations that we discussed earlier. It provides a means of writing special procedures, such as for updating, and someday its successor (TDMS) may provide decision-table input. A user can set up a data file rapidly, analyze the file, and get reports of the analysis — sometimes literally in minutes, if the data is available to the computer. If the user finds that he has made errors of omission or commission, he can correct those on the spot.

And just who is this "user"? He certainly does not have to be a programmer, as we have tried to indicate. The user is communicating with the computer via a high level language; a specialist in the jargon of the computer itself is not required here. (Programmers *are* needed to create the TSS-LUCID programs themselves, but are not needed in the use of those programs.) And perhaps not even a system analyst is required. The user might well be a line manager or an executive. There is another system (which we are not at liberty to discuss in detail) quite similar to TSS-LUCID that has been in operation at a large corporation for some time. The users are the line managers and executives. About one-quarter to one-third of the time, a manager or executive himself will sit at the console and interrogate the data file, as he is analyzing a problem. The rest of the time, he has his secretary enter a request for an already-defined report.

Time-sharing allows the user to set up a new system quickly and test it out. The test can be made with small volumes of data. Once the system has been checked out with this data, larger quantities of data can be added to the file. We see the time-sharing concept, complemented by the use of generalized file-processing routines and decision-table capabilities, greatly speeding up the process of converting an application to the computer.

The Meaning for Data-Processing Management

The major implications of the new technology are that many of today's decision-making methods (for data processing) are rapidly becoming obsolete — and data-processing management will have to change its methods accordingly.

Equipment Evaluation and Selection. This area is becoming so complex that mechanized evaluation appears to be the only realistic way of approaching the problem. Also, the evaluation must include not only the hardware but also its intimately related software, such as operating systems and program translators.

Software Selection. The selection of software really constitutes a new decision area, especially for a large number of medium and small installations. This decision becomes critical as alternative software packages become available. And the decision may become even more complex if hardware and software prices are separated — but in this case users may find it financially easier to obtain just the software they want.

Reduced Costs. With computing and data storage costs being reduced rapidly, formerly uneconomic applications can be considered for conversion to the computer. One such application is the retention of large volumes of detailed transaction data, for use by a management-reporting system. Also, new techniques can be considered, such as generalized file-processing routines. If these routines are somewhat less efficient in their use of computer time and storage — and this point is not conceded by the developers of these routines — this is becoming a matter of less importance.

New Implementation Methods. Generalized file processing routines, decision tables, application packages, and time-shared systems promise much greater speed and reduced costs for converting many applications to the computer. And another benefit, perhaps just as important, is that they will greatly ease the problem of making changes and improvements to applications already implemented by these methods.

Computing Utilities. It is quite possible that computing utilities will offer much more powerful hardware-software combinations than the vast majority of independent installations can support. If data processing management must choose between using a computing utility "now," which offers a powerful software system, or waiting several years before a more limited system is available for their own computer, we suspect that many users will sign up with the computing utilities. And they may well transfer more and more of their workload to these utilities, as they integrate applications using the new implementation methods. Finally the day may come when they decide to transfer all remaining workload to the utility, and get rid of their own computer. Small enterprises can gain the benefits of a large system at low cost by using a utility.

There will surely be resistance to the adoption of much of this new technology. Its adoption can affect jobs and prestige. The road to its use will be bumpy, as ever-possible troubles arise. But it will be up to data processing management to keep abreast of the changes in the technology, so that these changes can be incorporated into plans and methods as soon as practical.

6 Managing a Future EDP System

The process of managing and controlling an EDP system will change in many significant ways over the next ten years — because the nature of the EDP system itself will change. We have described some of these changes in previous chapters. Let us now consider a typical EDP system of the future, and the management implications it holds.

The system we visualize might be operated by a service organization, providing service to many user organizations on a demand basis. Or it might be the principal EDP installation of a corporation or Government activity. The system will be an on-line, time-shared system. Data will be fed into the system and obtained from the system through remote terminals. The system will also process batches of data where the response time can be relatively long. Regardless of whether the computer complex is located internally within one organization or whether it is a separate enterprise, we will call this service a "computing utility."

The equipment which forms the basis of the system will consist of one or more large, very high speed processors together with a number of storage units of varying capacity and access time. These processors and storage units will be interconnected to form a single processing system. The operating system software will determine which processors, storage units, and other devices are to be used at any given time.

The operating system will handle interruptions and will sequence jobs according to priority rules. It will handle the communication between the processors and input-output devices and will incorporate procedures for handling equipment failures. The users will have access to both privately developed and common data bases, under the control of the operating system; the operating system is thus charged with insuring against intrusion of privacy and against data destruction. The common data base will contain the files of information available for use by many users, as well as the computer programs available for general use. The private data bases will contain files against which the originators have placed restriction codes; use of such files — for inquiry or for updating — is limited under the control of the system.

People will use this system for a wide variety of data processing and computational tasks. Routine jobs such as payroll may still be processed through the batch features of the system. Changes to files and inquiries into files will be made through the terminals, where the user has the proper authority for such actions. Even some production processes might be controlled through on-line connections to the central computer. Some users will be debugging new programs. And some users will represent the computer system management, who will interact with the system to control its operation and to effect changes in the software structure and the data base organization.

Note that as far as such an EDP system is concerned, there are two main management aspects. One aspect is the management of the user's functions — the area to which the earlier portion of this book is addressed. These functions are much the same, whether the user has his own computer or is obtaining computing service from a utility. The other aspect is the management of the computing utility itself, the main subject of this chapter.

The Utility's Relations with its Customers

The management of the computing utility will be dealing with a wide variety of users. These users moreover will be in intimate contact with the hardware-software system, and will not be isolated from the system as are today's users of batch-type service bureaus. This means that the computing utility will have to provide "system managers" to act as advisors to the on-line users. These system managers will be skilled people, at least one of whom would always be on duty when the system is in operation. If a user is having trouble, a system manager would be signalled; he in turn can come on-line and ask if help is desired.

The system managers will have to provide for the education of almost any supervisory, managerial, or professional person in a user company — to aid them in feeding information into and getting information from the system. Where transaction data is being fed in on-line, the system managers may have to help a clerical-type person who is having trouble with the system. Clerks will have to be taught how to use the consoles and, in many cases, how to use the index to the common data base. Some users will want to learn how to program their own application programs.

Much of this education will be obtained through the computer system itself, by means of computer-assisted instruction. That is, there will be programs for the novice user which form a programmed course of instruction on how to use the computer system in a more sophisticated way. In some cases, the manufacturer of the computer may provide the software for these computer-assisted courses. In other cases, the utilities will have to develop such courses themselves.

In order to facilitate the use of the system by a variety of users, the utility will have to establish and insist upon the full adherence to various standards. There will be standards for the use of consoles. There will be standards for the way in which data can be identified. There will be standards for the programming languages which may be used for the preparation of application programs.

Users will be developing programs of all sorts for their own use. Programs may be shared between different groups — and this intergroup use of programs requires control. For example, a production-control center may develop very complex programs for the scheduling of manufacturing work orders in one division of a company. The question then arises: should these programs be entered into the common data base so that they can be used by other divisions of the company? The incorporation of a program into the common data base is a change equivalent to the modification of the equipment. Careful review and analysis of the system implications of such a change will have to be made before the new programs can be accepted into the common data base. Let us emphasize, though, that this control does not prevent any user from building his own private files and programs.

In order to control changes to the data base, change control procedures will have to be adopted. A major function of the utility's operations group will be the recognition, analysis, coordination, and introduction of changes into the common data base.

Placing data, even for private use, into a major computer system brings up the question of data security. As time goes on and experience is gained with these systems, users will find it desirable to put even proprietary data, politically sensitive data, or personally sensitive data into such a system. Likewise, certain programs that contain procedures which give an organization a competitive advantage and which it therefore considers proprietary will be stored in such a system. Thus, there is need to assure the user that certain kinds of data can be kept securely in the system, and can be called for only by the originator or his delegates. With the present state of the art, there are some techniques which will give some degree of assurance that this kind of security has been provided. Systems can be designed to make it quite difficult for one remote user to gain access to another user's data. To date, however, there is no way of insuring that the system manager or his staff cannot obtain any of the data in the system.

System development is required if utilities are to provide the necessary security for the most sensitive data. We know of one case where one of the processors of a system, and some of the memory units and peripheral storage units, were designed so that they could be completely disconnected from the main processing system by a series of swtches. These switches were physically under the control of the user. That user could operate the switches to separate an entire subsystem for use in processing his own sensitive data, with good assurance that no one else could get at the data at the time it was being processed. This solution, however, has its disadvantages, since it depends upon physical access to part of the equipment system and possibly could not be used for any significant number of users.

In addition to the data security problem, its converse also exists: the need to audit or review data that is being processed for other people. Certified public accountants, internal auditors, and other auditing agencies will want to review transactions, the data files, and the programs that are being used by certain organizations. The utility may have to provide software to make it possible to carry out auditing techniques such as random sampling of certain transactions and data files. The auditing agencies will want to determine the specific sampling techniques they will use, but the utility's software system must permit such techniques within its general framework.

We have said previously that many users will want to develop their own applications programs, in line with current trends. The utility will thus have to provide support for users in the form of consultation on programming techniques and usage. And there may be cases where the utility's staff will be called upon to make at least minor changes to a user's program — which step obviously has many perils. Very careful management is required to be sure that there is good coordination and cooperation between the user's staff and the utility's staff, especially in cases where errors or difficulties are encountered.

As we also mentioned earlier, utilities will be faced with the problem of peak loads. Electric utilities, for example, solve this problem by building more capacity than they will need on the average, and also by providing interconnections with other neighboring electric utilities. Through these interconnections, the utilities can buy and sell electricity to each other, as one means of solving their individual peak-load problems. The computing utilities may adopt these same solutions where possible. For instance, it would be feasible for a computing utility to transmit computation problems and program compilations to a neighboring utility, to be processed and sent back. But where a mass of data must be transmitted — such as the need to transmit whole data files — to the other utility, this solution may be impractical.

There is still another solution to the peak-load problem that the computing utility might well adopt: the use of priorities. In the case of the telephone system, for example, the priority system is primarily "first come, first served." When the number you want is busy, you get a busy signal. But with the logic available to the computing utility, more sophisticated priorities could be used. At Project MAC at M.I.T., for instance, a priority system has been used in which the people with the longer processing jobs are assigned longer response times. Since these people normally expect to wait some time for their results, they will be less annoyed by a longer response time than people making simple inquiries or having jobs with a small amount of processing. But there will be pressure to use priority systems that imply a value judgment — such as giving a higher priority to inquiries by top executives than to office staff members who are answering customer inquiries. Such systems can generate a host of problems. Management of the utility *must* be deeply involved in establishing the priority rules for the users of an on-line time-shared system.

Charging for Service. This question of priorities is closely related to the question of charging the users for the computer service. In many current installations, the cost of operating the computer system and the cost of the related software are charged to an overhead account, so that the users view the system as a "free" service. Other organizations charge individual users (departments, projects, etc.) for the use of the computer, often on the basis of hourly charges. In the case of utility systems, the same choices are available — overhead or direct charges. If the user is to be charged for time used, then the software system must keep track of this time, and this turns out to be no simple matter. As data characters are entered via a console, the computer is interrupted for perhaps only a few microseconds — to check the validity of the character and perhaps put it away in its proper place in a message. When the message is complete, it must be analyzed and appropriate action taken. Some jobs will make extensive use of the more costly internal memory of the computer — and probably should be charged for the amount of memory used as well as the length of time used. The same logic applies to the other equipment used — external storage such as magnetic tapes or mass storage, card readers, printers, etc. In any case, the rates charged must have sufficient provision for overhead in them to permit the utility to develop software systems and do the equipment planning and maintenance necessary to carry on its activities.

Additional proposals have been made to use the rates charged for computer service as the method of setting priority. Charges might be higher for fast response time than for more leisurely responses. In effect, this is equivalent to giving priority to those who are willing to pay for rapid service. Such a procedure might not always be in the best interest of the over-all organization. For instance, an organization might have a specially-funded research project with a limited budget where fast response can aid significantly in completing the project, and where the payoff from success can be very large. On the other hand, the manager of a successful operating division might easily pay for very fast response to his inquiries when, in fact, he may not really need such a fast response. We foresee, therefore, that the priority system and method of charging will probably be a complex structure where the charges for fast response generally will be higher. But there will also be a variety of classes of service, as well as provision for high priorities at low cost, for those cases where the over-all organization will benefit.

In addition to fast response service, jobs that lend themselves to batch processing can be processed in a utility just as they are in present batch processing systems. The utility's operating software probably will be designed so that whenever there are no on-line users, the system will process batched jobs. In fact, batch jobs can be given priority over some on-line jobs when necessary to meet deadlines. The opration still involves scheduling of batch processing activities and requires the same liaison with batch users. The major differences from the way that batch jobs are handled today will be that batch jobs usually will have a lower priority than on-line jobs (so that scheduling becomes less certain) and the entire batch processing activity becomes a small part of a much larger operating environment.

Operations Management Considerations

We have alluded to the fact that the software and the data files will require careful attention and control. The utility's staff will be faced with the problem of finding and correcting errors both in the software and in the data files — particularly in the common data base. This staff will have to develop standards for using the system, insure adherence to them, and disseminate the standards and related educational material. The staff will have to concern itself with the growth of the system and plan for increases in system capacity. This staff will often detect the need for hardware or software system changes, in the course of their observing the daily service of customer requests. To control change, utility management must develop and use an effective means of change control, for changes both to the software and to the data files. If changes are made without good change control, at the very least the introduction of later changes will be more difficult. Even worse, it is likely that user operation of the system will be curtailed, due to unexpected effects of some changes.

The utility's operating staff will probably work in a hectic environment, much like the environment of today's engineering and scientific computer installations that run hundreds of different jobs per shift. Such an operation must be managed by a forceful yet technically knowledgeable manager. This manager will probably divide his staff into several parts. One group will be in charge of operations and possibly maintenance. If the equipment maintenance is provided by the computer manufacturer, then this staff will perform liaison between the utility and the manufacturer. One key function in this regard will be that of scheduling the maintenance to provide the least disruption of customer services — a problem, in a sense, like trying to repair a jet airplane while the plane is in flight. The maintenance must be performed on schedule and it must be of high quality so that the equipment malfunctions cannot plague the installation.

The operation of the equipment probably will not involve too much that is new, in relation to today's installations. For batch-type jobs card loading, tape handling, and printer handling will probably be required. But many of the operator functions will be handled by the software. One operational function alluded to earlier is that of the system managers, who will be always on hand observing the operation of the system and helping users when necessary.

Another major group will be the software and data base maintenance group. This group will consist of programming experts who are adept at finding and correcting difficulties — often on the basis of meager evidence. The systems programmers in this group should be sensitive to user needs, as well as to the software needs of the utility itself. The data specialists in this group should be expert in file organization and the ways in which data can move between the different levels of data storage. The maintenance of software and data files will be difficult in a time-shared system since it is almost impossible to recreate the exact conditions that caused the error.

The creation of new software, as well as customer-requested programming, probably will be performed by a third group of people. Finally, it appears likely that a utility will want to have a research group whose job it will be to find system improvements through simulation studies and the continual review of operating statistics and procedures.

Design Considerations

A major function of the utility's staff will be to plan for adding increments of processing and storage capacity. It will be difficult to predict requirement accurately, particularly in the early years of life of these utilities. Specifications must be written and negotiations must be conducted to acquire the necessary equipment. Also, it must be possible for the software systems to handle the expanded capacity. The new increments of hardware must be added without interrupting service to the on-line users. For some increments of capacity, parts of the data base may have to be relocated, perhaps causing additional complexities to the implementation.

This need for continual enhancement points up a challenging problem for the utilities — the need for continued compatibility of hardware. Compatibility has *not* been a major characteristic of the computer field to date; every new computer seems to have is own peculiar characteristics. The third generation of computers incorporate more interfamily compatibility — and some intrafamily compatibility — than the computer field has previously witnessed. But time alone will tell how much compatibility will be retained in the computers five years hence. If the computing utilities become a major force in the field — as we believe they will — they will demand a high degree of compatibility. A utility just could not afford to go through a major reprogramming effort every few years when it added new equipment.

Another function of the utility's staff will be to analyze the possibilities of, and devolop plans for, a complete failure of the system. Many such systems *must* operate on a twenty-four-hour-per-day, seven-day-per-week basis, just like the electrical utilities — though not all system components need be in operation at times of low demand, such as on weekends or at night. If a number of interconnected computing utilities all failed at one time — as happened to the electrical utilities in New York and New England in late 1965 — a catastrophe of considerable magnitude would develop.

In order to maintain twenty-four-hour operation in the face of unscheduled failures and maintenance requirements, the software operating system must be carefully designed, hopefully to provide "graceful degradation"; that is, the system should continue to operate, although at a lower level of efficiency, even when major units are out of operation. Furthermore, the software system should be able to recognize the failure and reorganize its processing and storage procedures to account for the failure. This graceful degradation is on the verge of becoming a reality in some military and air-traffic-control systems today, although it is posing some challenging hardware and software problems. Further complications are involved in developing procedures to return the unit to service after it has been repaired. Storage units offer particular difficulties. If a storage unit has failed, there must be some way to recover the data which should have been stored therein and then to continue operating.

Another factor in achieving twenty-four-hour operation is the need for redundant equipment, not only for operating under conditions of random breakdown, but also for handling routine preventive maintenance. A computer installation often has a multiplicity of peripheral units, particularly magnetic-tape units; utilities will probably be the same. Peripheral units can be taken off the system and maintained on a preventive basis without too much difficulty, most likely during periods of low workload. The same philosophy must also be applied to the central processors and storage units. This implies that an around-the-clock utility will need at least two processors, so that one can be maintained while the other handles the load. Storage units present an even more difficult problem if they contain any part of the permanent data base. Interchangeable magnetic disks and decks of magnetic cards, as currently in use, offer a solution to the problem of switching a data base to an operable unit.

Another factor involved in twenty-four-hour operation is the fact that system control becomes a major responsibility that involves more than just minute-by-minute activity. Things are happening so fast inside the computer that a human "controller" can detect only the most gross discrepancies. In essence, the hardware-software system must control itself, reporting any unusual conditions that are detected to the human system manager. Unusual conditions would include extra heavy workloads, unusual equipment failures, equipment errors, and so on.

As we discussed earlier, another partial means for obtaining twenty-four-hour service is through the interconnection of computing utilities. The problems of maintaining a utility's data base while it is out of operation appear severe, and their solution will require a major development effort. Also, the communications costs for the interconnection of utilities will not be trivial.

Summary

It seems to us that the computing utility will come to dominate the computing field, perhaps by the mid-1970's — in contrast to today's situation where most user groups have their own installations. The utility concept gives the user access to a more powerful hardware-software combination than he can generally afford on his own. It should be noted once again that, in our use of the term "utility," a large organization might well have its own utility. There is no implication that the utility must be a separate organization.

The arrival of the computing utility will not change the user's data processing functions substantially. There still will be the need to plan the future data processing program, to organize the effort and to staff the effort. If anything, the arrival of the computing utility will accentuate the management problems we have discussed in this book because they will probably bring sophisticated systems to the user at an early date. The fact that the computer operations will not be located in the user's data processing function is really not an important point, as long as the user's requirements are met.

On the other hand, we have tried to point out that the computing utilities will not easily come into existence. They are faced with many problems, some of which we have discussed. And there are legal problems, too; since the "public" computing utilities will be providing a public service, it would seem likely that they will become subject to governmental regulation just like other forms of utilities. And a whole new body of legal knowledge is sure to develop. Add to these problems the rather severe technological requirements imposed by the computing utilities and it is clear that they will not "take over" from the individual installations in the immediate future. But they are becoming a significant factor in the field.

We began this book with the statement that the transition to the third generation of computers — including the computing utilities — appears to us to be a potentially greater jump than was the transition from tabulating machines to computers, or between the first and second generations of computers. This is not just because of the hardware advances — although these are important.

But it is also due to the state of the art that has been reached, in software, applications packages, and sophisticated uses. All of these things tie together to provide the user with a much more powerful tool than he has had previously with computers.

The increased sophistication of use and the rapid change in the state of the art will pose a severe challenge to data processing management. The methods that have been used for managing the data processing operation in the past will not — in many cases — meet the requirements of tomorrow. Top managements can no longer remain so aloof of the computer, the goals of data processing, and the staff organization. Data processing management cannot continue to rely on the staff selection methods, project organization methods, and program guidance methods that have typically been used in the past. Now is the time to prepare for this new environment that will be on us before the decade is out.

Selected Bibliography and Notes

Chapter 1

[1] R. L. Sisson and R. G. Canning, *A Manager's Guide to Computer Systems,* Wiley (1967). This volume complements and precedes the present volume.

[2] Generalizations in this chapter on the history of the computer field and in Chapter 3 on the discussion of data processing job functions have been drawn from an extensive review of the literature. See *Data Processing Digest,* 1955 to the present (1140 S. Robertson Blvd., Los Angeles, Calif.). (The authors were the founders and original publishers of *Data Processing Digest* and were thus exposed to the bulk of the literature over this time period.)

[3] Concerning correlations in programmer's aptitude testing, see the note under Chapter 4.

Chapter 2

[4] R. L. Ackoff and P. Rivett, *A Manager's Guide to Operations Research,* Wiley (1963). This volume gives a good description of the potentials of O.R. and how a company can go about using it.

[5] For a discussion of planning in the context of the Department of Defense methods, including the planning-programming-budgeting system, see
    (a) D. J. Smalter and R. L. Ruggles, Jr., "Six Business Lessons from The Pentagon," *Harvard Business Review,* March–April 1966, 64–75.
    (b) D. Seligman, "McNamara's Management Revolution," *Fortune,* July 1965, 117ff.
    (c) E. S. Quade, *Analysis for Military Decisions,* Rand McNally (1966).
    (d) "Computer-Assisted Corporate Planning," *EDP Analyzer,* September 1966 (134 Escondido Avenue, Vista, Calif. 92083).

[6] For a discussion of the use of PERT-type networks in planning, see:
    (a) R. L. Martino, *Finding the Critical Path,* American Management Association, 1964.

(b) R. L. Martino, *Applied Operational Planning,* American Management Association, 1964.

(c) L. S. Hill, "Some Cost Accounting Problems in PERT Cost," *Journal of Industrial Engineering,* February 1966, 87–91,

(d) "How Useful Are PERT-type Networks?" *EDP Analyzer,* August 1964.

[7] For an interesting approach to EDP system design, see "Study Organization Plan," a series of pamphlets published by IBM in 1963; particularly see the discussion of Phase 1.

[8] A. Ginsberg, H. M. Markowitz, and P. M. Oldfather, "Programming by Questionnaire," Report AD 613 976, Clearinghouse for Federal Scientific and Technical Information; (Springfield, Va. 22151), price $3.00. This report discusses the generalized job-shop model developed at the Rand Corporation.

[9] For a discussion of the benefits of the corporate data file, as well as the imposing magnitude of the task of creating it, see the November and December 1966 issues of *EDP Analyzer.*

[10] For a discussion of data processing planning in the context discussed in this chapter, see "Planning for Data Processing," *EDP Analyzer,* June 1966.

Chapter 3

[11] M. H. Schwartz, "Organization and Administration of Electronic Data Processing: A Functional Approach," talk given in September 1964. For a copy, write to the author, Research and Development Dept., First National City Bank, 399 Park Avenue, New York, N.Y.

[12] R. Tannenbaum, "Overcoming Barriers to the Acceptance of New Ideas and Methods." This paper is included as Appendix I in *Electronic Data Processing for Business and Industry,* by R. G. Canning, Wiley (1956).

[13] For a discussion of how design sessions can be conducted, see "Time to Consider Decision Structure Tables and Design Sessions," *EDP Analyzer,* May 1963.

Chapter 4

[14] Generalizations on data processing staff's efforts to upgrade themselves have been made on the basis of the authors' experiences in teaching, as well as participating in a number of technical societies, some since the early 1950's; these societies include the Association for Computing Machinery, Institute of Electrical and Electronic Engineers, American Institute of Industrial Engineers, Systems and Procedures Association, The Institute of Management Sciences, Operations Research Society of America, and the Data Processing Management Association. Experiences have ranged from attending many meetings and conferences to program planning.

[15] Many studies have reported on the (low) correlations between programmer's aptitude test results and supervisors' ratings on performance; for instance, see:

    (a) Reinstedt, Hammidi, Peres, and Richard, "Programmer Performance Prediction Study," The Rand Corporation, March 1964 (1700 Main Street, Santa Monica, Calif.).

    (b) Dallis K. Perry, A number of reports on programmer-selection testing covering the past several years. System Development Corp., 2500 Colorado Avenue, Santa Monica, Calif.

[16] For information on the DPMA Certificate in Data Processing, write to Data Processing Management Association, 505 Busse Highway, Park Ridge, Ill. 60068.

[17] For statistics on educational backgrounds in the data processing field, see H. Roemmich, "A Descriptive Analysis of Candidates for the 1966 CDP Examination," *DPMA Quarterly* (see DPMA address above), October 1966, 2–25.

[18] For a discussion of the use of consulting services, see:

    (a) W. Seney, *Effective Use of Business Consultants,* Financial Executives Research Foundation (50 West 44th St., New York).

    (b) "Effective Use of EDP Services," *EDP Analyzer,* April 1965.

Chapter 5

[19] For more information on mechanized computer evaluations, see D. J. Herman and F. C. Ihrer, "The Use of a Computer to Evaluate Computers," *Proceedings of the 1964 Spring Joint Computer Conference,* Spartan Books, Washington, D.C., or write to Comress, Inc., 2120 Blandesburg Road N.E., Washington, D. C. 20018.

[20] For information on the *Auerbach Standard EDP Reports,* write to Auerbach Info, Inc., 121 N. Broad Street, Philadelphia, Pa. 19107.

[21] The following issues of *EDP Analyzer* are related to the subjects discussed in this chapter: "Generalized File Processing Software" (October 1965), "Coming Changes in System Analysis and Design" (November 1965), "Time to Consider Decision Structure Tables and Design Sessions" (May 1963), "How to Use Decision Tables" (May 1966), "The Changing Computer Market" (April 1966), "The Changing Software Market" (July 1966), and "Application Packages: Coming Into Their Own" (July 1967).

Chapter 6

[22] D. F. Parkhill, *The Challenge of the Computer Utility,* Addison-Wesley (1966), the first book devoted to a discussion of the computing utility.

[23] R. M. Fano, "The MAC System: the Computer Utility Approach," *IEEE Spectrum,* January 1965, 56–64 (345 East 47th St., New York, N.Y. 10017). This article gives a good overview of the important Project MAC at M.I.T., plus a good bibliography on the subject of time-sharing.

Selected Glossary

Application package. A group of generalized programs designed to perform a specific application (such as payroll); a user selects options to adapt the package to his specific needs.

Assembler. A computer program used for translating a programmer's language into the machine language; usually one machine instruction is generated for each of the programmer's instructions.

Batch processing. A technique by which the transactions to be processed are collected into a group prior to processing; the processing of the transactions is thus delayed until the batch is formed.

COBOL. The Common Business Oriented Language, for programming business applications, which may be used with most medium- and larger-size business computers.

Compiler. A translator program for translating a (higher level) programmer's language—such as COBOL—into machine language; normally several machine instructions are generated for each programmer's instruction.

Computing utility. An on-line, time-shared computer complex serving many remote users; see chapters 5 and 6.

Data retrieval. The retrieval of records, or selected portions of records, from a data file, where the contents of those records meet specified criteria.

Decision tables. A simple tabular method for expressing complex condition-action relationships; methods are available for converting some types of decision tables directly into computer programs; see Chapter 5 for an illustration.

Direct access storage. See Mass storage.

FORTRAN. FORmula TRANslation; a family of higher-level programming languages used primarily for engineering and scientific applications.

Generations (of computers). A rather arbitrary classification of computers according to some of their design characteristics; the first generation is considered to be vacuum-tube machines built prior to 1960. The second generation is considered to be transistor machines built during the period 1960 to 1965, while the third generation uses integrated or hybrid circuitry with delivery starting about 1965. Characteristics other than type of circuitry are involved, such as the size of internal memory, data-communications ability, etc.

Generalized file-processing software. These generalized programs perform the common file-processing functions such as file creation, file maintenance, selection, extraction and reporting—functions which represent a good portion of most business-type programs; see Chapter 5.

G. I. S. Generalized Information System, a system of generalized file-processing software developed by IBM.

Hardware. This term means just what it says; as far as computers are concerned, it means the physical product delivered by the computer manufacturers, such as central processing units, mass storage, tape units, etc. It is differentiated from "software," defined below.

IMRADS. Information Management Retrieval and Dissemination System, a system of generalized file-processing software developed by Univac.

INFOL. A generalized information-storage-and-retrieval language developed by Control Data Corporation.

I. D. S. Integrated Data Store, a generalized information-storage-and-retrieval system developed by GE and embedded in the COBOL language.

Internal memory. The high-speed storage unit(s) attached to the central processor in which are stored the programs and data currently being processed.

Mass storage. This term generally is applied to very large-volume storage (from millions to billions of characters) where any portion of the storage can be accessed in less than one second. Synonymous terms include direct-access storage and random-access storage.

Multiprocessing. Although several definitions are in use for this term, the most commonly used meaning is two or more central processing units sharing a common internal memory and sharing a common workload.

Multiprogramming. As most commonly used, the term means the ability of a central processing unit to work on two or more programs "concurrently"—that is, working on one until some form of interruption occurs to cause the computer to work on another program.

On-line. Input-output units (consoles, terminals, etc.) are considered to be on-line if they have a direct connection with the central processing unit, as opposed to converting data to machine language and storing it in punched cards or paper tape, for later entry into the computer.

Operating system. The master control program residing in the computer for handling many of the operating functions—sequencing of jobs, checking for input and output data errors and taking corrective action when such errors are located, job accounting, etc.

PL/1. Programming Language 1, a new programming language, the specifications for which were released by IBM at the same time that the IBM 360 was announced; it combines features of other high-level languages such as COBOL, FORTRAN and Algol.

Random access storage. See Mass storage.

SCERT. Systems and Computers Evaluation and Review Technique; a set of proprietary computer programs developed by Comress, Inc. of Washington, D. C., for the mechanized evaluation of computers.

Software. This term was originally coined to identify the computer programs provided without additional charge by the computer manufacturers (as differentiated from hardware); such programs were usually general purpose so as to be useful to a large class of users. Lately, the term has been broadened to include all computer programs.

Terminal. A device for entering information into a computer, usually by means of a keyboard, and for receiving and displaying information from the computer, usually by means of a printing mechanism (as in a teletypewriter) or on a cathode-ray tube.

Time-shared system. A hardware-software system capable of multiprogramming (see above) and connected to a number of remote on-line terminals (also see definitions above); in addition, the operating system allocates short "slices of time" to each user, in the order of microseconds or milliseconds. Generally, when a user's time slice is used up, his job goes into the waiting line for a fraction of a second until its turn comes up again.

Translator. Similar to assembler and compiler; a program for converting between one language (most often, the language used by a programmer) and another language (most often, the machine language).

Index

Italic numbers indicate principal citation.